DURVAL DE NORONHA GOYOS JR.

THE CAMPAIGN OF THE BRAZILIAN EXPEDITIONARY FORCE FOR THE LIBERATION OF ITALY

Translated by Fernanda Pinheiro, Philip Badiz, Robert Williams, under the co-ordination of the author

CULTURA ACADÊMICA
Editora

© 2014 Durval de Noronha Goyos Jr.
The moral rights of the author have been asserted.

Cultura Acadêmica
Praça da Sé, 108
01001-900, São Paulo, SP, Brazil
Phone: 55 (11) 3242-7171
Fax: 55 (11) 3242-7172
www.culturaacademica.com.br
feu@editora.unesp.br

Cataloging in Publication(CIP) data

G745c

Goyos Júnior, Durval de Noronha
   The campaign of the brazilian expeditionary force for the liberation of Italy / Durval de Noronha Goyos Jr. ; translation Fernanda Pinheiro , Philip Badiz , Robert Williams. – 1. ed. – São Paulo : Cultura Acadêmica, 2014.
   il.; 21 cm.

   Translation of: *A campanha da força expedicionária brasileira pela libertação da Itália*
   ISBN 978-85-7983-544-5

   1. Brazil. Army. Brazilian Expeditionary Force. 2 World War, 1939-1945 – Brazil. 3 Brazil – Politics and government.

14-15057   CDD: 981.06
                                              CDU: 94(81).082/.083

Affiliated publishers:

Dedicated to Sargent Ruy de Noronha Goyos, of the 6th Engineer Battalion of the Brazilian Expeditionary Force (FEB), on his one hundredth birthday.

Chronology

28th October 1922 – Benito Mussolini forms a coalition government in Italy.

30th October 1930 – President Washington Luís is overthrown by an armed movement led by Getúlio Vargas.

9th July 1932 – The Constitutionalist Revolution is launched in São Paulo.

30th January 1933 – Adolf Hitler is appointed German Prime Minister.

17th July 1934 – The Constitution of 1934 is sanctioned in Brazil.

27th November 1935 – A communist conspiracy fails in Rio de Janeiro.

5th May 1936 – Fascist Italian troops occupy Addis Ababa, the capital of Ethiopia.

8 DURVAL DE NORONHA GOYOS JR.

7th July 1937 – Marco Polo bridge Incident, in China, and the Japanese invasion of Manchuria. The Second World War begins.

10th November 1937 – Coup by Getúlio Vargas, inauguration of the Estado Novo and promulgation of the 1937 Constitution in Brazil.

12th March 1938 – Germany promotes unification with Austria, Anschluss.

11th May 1938 – The Integralist uprising fails in Rio de Janeiro.

30th September 1938 – Germany absorbs the Sudetenland in Czechoslovakia.

15th March 1939 – Germany incorporates Czechoslovakia.

23rd August 1939 – Germany and the Soviet Union celebrate a non-aggression pact.

1st September 1939 – Invasion of Poland by Nazi forces.

3rd September 1939 – Britain and France declare war on Germany. The European phase of the Second World War begins.

4th September 1939 – Beginning of British naval blockade of Germany begins.

17th September 1939 – Soviet troops invade Poland.

9th April 1940 – Germany invades Denmark and Norway.

10th May 1940 – Germany invades France, Belgium and Luxembourg. Winston Churchill is appointed British Prime Minister.

10th June 1940 – Italy attacks the United Kingdom and France.

14th June 1940 – Nazi troops occupy Paris.

18th June 1940 – General Charles de Gaulle forms the French government in exile in London, United Kingdom.

22nd September 1940 – Japan occupies Vietnam.

30th September 1940 – Germany, Italy and Japan celebrate the Axis Treaty.

28th October 1940 – Italy attacks Greece.

31st March 1941 – The German offensive begins in North Africa.

6th April 1941 – Germany attacks Yugoslavia and Greece.

5th May 1941 – Germany establishes a submarine base in Dakar, Senegal, for engagement operations in the battle of the South Atlantic.

22nd June 1941 – Adolf Hitler begins Operation Barbarossa and invades the Union of Soviet Socialist Republics (USSR).

9th August 1941 – Roosevelt promotes the Atlantic Charter in meeting with Churchill, listing basic values.

23rd November 1941 – Italy is defeated by British troops in Ethiopia and Somalia.

7th December 1941 – Japan attacks U.S. bases in Pearl Harbour, Hawaii.

8th December 1941 – The United States declares war on the Empire of Japan.

25th December 1941 – Hong Kong, a British colony, surrenders to Japanese troops.

1st January 1942 – The allies endorse the UN Declaration.

28th January 1942 – Meeting of North American Foreign Ministers in Rio de Janeiro. Brazil severs relations with the Axis States and Germany declares belligerence against Brazil.

15th February 1942 – Singapore surrenders to Japanese troops.

2nd March 1942 – An Air Base is established in Parnamirim, Natal, Rio Grande do Norte .

3rd March 1942 – Brazil and the United States sign a Lend-Lease agreement.

11th March 1942 – Japan conquers the Philippines, New Guinea, Java and Burma.

15th August 1942 – German submarines sink six Brazilian merchant ships in the northeast of the country.

31st August 1942 – Brazil declares war on Germany and Italy.

14th January 1943 – Strategic meeting in Casablanca between Roosevelt, Churchill and Stalin.

28th January 1943 – President Getulio Vargas meets with President Franklin Roosevelt in Natal, Rio Grande do Norte.

31st January 1943 – Nazi forces surrender to the Red Army in Stalingrad.

9th August 1943 – The Brazilian Expeditionary Force (*Força Expedicionária Brasileira*, FEB) is created.

3rd September 1943 – Allied forces land in Calabria, southern Italy.

8th September 1943 – The Italian government signs an armistice with the Allies.

7th October 1943 - The Division General João Batista Mascarenhas de Moraes is appointed commander of the FEB.

23rd November 1943 – Summit in Cairo between Roosevelt, Churchill and Chiang Kai-shek.

28th November 1943 – Summit in Tehran between Stalin, Roosevelt and Churchill.

5th June 1944 – Liberation of Rome by the Allies.

6th June 1944 – Allied Invasion of Normandy.

30th June 1944 – FEB ships out from Rio de Janeiro for operations in the Italian theatre of war.

1st July 1944 – The Bretton Woods Conference begins, in New Hampshire USA.

25th August 1944 – Liberation of Paris by Allied forces, with Free French troops at the forefront.

10th September 1944 –The First Air Force Fighter Division of the Brazilian Air Force (*Força Aérea Brasileira*, FAB) begins operations in Italy.

16th September 1944 – The artillery of the FEB enters into action. The first of 50 cities of strategic importance, Massarosa, is liberated by the FEB.

17th January 1945 – Liberation of Warsaw by the Red Army.

4th February 1945 – Yalta strategic summit between Stalin, Roosevelt and Churchill.

21st February 1945 – FEB takes Monte Castelo with the support of the First Air Force Fighter Division of the FAB.

13th March 1945 – Occupation of Vienna by the Red Army.

14th April 1945 – The FEB liberates Montese and fraternizes with local residents.

26th April 1945 – FEB accepts the surrender of the German 148th Division, with 21,000 combatants.

28th April 1945 – Benito Mussolini is shot by the resistance in northern Italy.

1st May 1945 – Adolf Hitler commits suicide in his bunker in Berlin.

8th May 1945 – Germany surrenders unconditionally to the Allies.

26th June 1945 – The UN Charter is signed.

2nd September 1945 – Japan surrenders unconditionally to the Allies.

29th October 1945 – A military coup overthrows Getúlio Vargas.

2nd December 1945 – Democratic elections are held in Brazil.

2nd June 1946 – Proclamation of the Republic of Italy.

18th September 1946 – The Democratic Constitution is promulgated in Brazil.

INDEX OF IMAGES

Mussolini in his prime   40

Hitler takes Paris   52

President Getúlio Vargas   70

Chancellor Osvaldo Aranha   71

German colonies in Brazil   78

Naval warfare on the Brazilian coast   84

Ensign of the FEB   109

The FEB campaign in Italy   110

General Mascarenhas de Moraes, Commander
of the FEB   111

Sergeant Ruy de Noronha Goyos, of the 6th Engineer
Battalion of the FEB   112

Sergeant Ruy de Noronha Goyos and companions in
Monte Castelo   113

Ensign of the 1st Air Force Fighter Group of the FAB   114

Febiano, private Menasses Barros de Aguiar in
   training before shipping to Italy   114

First Lieutenant Artillery Rubens Resstel   115

Captain Plínio Pitaluga   116

Ensign of the UN   127

SUMMARY

Foreword   17
Introduction   23

1 Fascist Italy   29
2 Nazi Germany   41
3 Aspects of Brazil in the late 1930s and the
   early 1940s   53
4 The coastal defence of Brazil and maritime
   and aerial war in the South Atlantic   73
5 The FEB Campaign in Italy   85
6 Epilogue   117

Afterword   129
References   135
Index   141
About the Author   147

FOREWORD

Sergio Xavier Ferolla[1]

Representing an auspicious fact, due to its rarity in the academic sphere in our country, particularly for Brazilians attentive to the correct framework of actions of national interest, we welcome this precious essay by a acknowledged intellectual and renowned exponent in the national and international legal universe.

This relevant and patriotic message framed by bonds of precious historical value was presented at the opening of the traditional Italian Week. As the son of an Italian mother and dual citizen of Brazil and Italy Dr. Durval de Noronha Goyos, as guest speaker, saw fit to masterfully highlight the remarkable contribution that the campaign of the *Força Expedicionária Brasileira* (FEB, Brazilian Expeditionary Force) represented in

---

1 Sergio Xavier Ferolla is Lieutenant-Air-Brigadier and Judge Advocate of the General Courts-Martial.

the promotion of the rule of law, the observance of human rights and the prevalence of democratic order on a global scale.

In the late 1950s, when I began my career as a Flying officer, integrating the ranks of pilots of the First Fighter Aviation Group, among my instructors and commanders were some of the heroic fighters that registered a strong presence in the skies of Italy, such as Hélio Langsch Keller, group commander; Camera Fortunato de Oliveira, eminent cartoonist and creator of the ostrich symbol; Rui Moreira Lima, the author of *Senta a pua* [lit. Full power] (2001), among many others. Venerable men, with the utmost respect and admiration for the young lieutenants, who transmitted to younger officers their combat experience and the *esprit de corps* that united everyone on land and in the air. With satisfaction, they reported the harmonious and joyful experience they shared with the civilian population and the welcoming refuge that many received from the Italian resistance fighters, the *partigiani*, preventing their imprisonment, when their plane was shot down in territory held by the enemy.

Important actors in the struggle to dismantle the fascist regime in Italy, where they were received with ardent sympathy by the oppressed segment of the population, both on the ground and in the air, and far and beyond the bloody battles, the heroic Brazilian fighters laid the groundwork so that on the 2nd June 1946, the referendum could take place, in which the Italian people chose the end of the monarchy and the subsequent establishment of the Italian Republic.

With his meticulous and well-documented approach, the author leads the reader on a historic step regarding the military, social and economic events that would lead the nations to the cataclysm of World War II, in which millions of lives were brutally ended.

The political/military earthquake that involved all humankind maximised ideological radicalism with its political and economic interests in all regions of the globe. Particularly in Europe, the redefinition of new territorial boundaries established a clear bipartition, leaving the Eastern nations forcibly amalgamated under the dominion of communist Russia, while the west of the continent followed the policy dictated by the United States of America. The so-called "Cold War" was presented as the new threat to humanity.

On every continent, this bipolarity reconciled a pernicious scenario and, transmuting into new features and artifices of domination, localised military confrontations and economic disputes that benefit the strongest are stimulated by the holders of terrible weapons of destruction.

In 1971, speaking to the trainees of *Escola Superior de Guerra* (War College), Araújo Castro, then ambassador of Brazil in Washington, emphasised that

> on various occasions, within the setting of the United Nations, before the General Assembly and before the Economic and Social Council, Brazil has sought to characterise what is now clearly looming as a firm undisguised trend towards the freezing of world power. And when we speak of power, we speak not only of military power, but also of political power, of economic power, of scientific and technical power.

In a global scenario, the influence on the economy and on finances led to an uncontrolled model of open markets, principally aimed at maximising profits and control in countries seeking development and, therefore, dependent on economic and technological resources. However, the voracity of the deified market extended its ills to all humankind, culminating in a systemic crisis in all sectors of the economy and the collapse of the international financial institutions.

The crisis, which continues to persist in the first decade of the twenty-first century, created an environment of despair and public outcry in numerous countries, with particular emphasis on the European continent, and may lead to worrisome scenarios in social and economic fields. The leaders who conduct actions in search of the recovery of shattered economies should keep in mind the premonitory statements of the great English economist John Maynard Keynes (2002), when commenting on the Treaty of Versailles in 1919, he concluded that

> Men will not always die quietly. For starvation, which brings to some lethargy and a helpless despair, drives other temperaments to the nervous instability of hysteria and to a mad despair. And these in their distress may overturn the remnants of organisation and submerge civilisation itself in their attempts to satisfy desperately the overwhelming needs of the individual.

The shock of the economic catastrophe recorded in 2008 has imposed the presence of the State, such that it is no longer considered a cardinal sin by renowned neoliberal thinkers, who engage in the defence of the injection of considerable resources into the sectors of manufacturing, services and the "sacrilege" of state intervention in the sacred temples of finance of the moribund international economy.

Our country, due to the greatness of its people, has overcome obstacles that have been interposed in its historical walk and, with effort and perseverance, will reach the goal of a great and just nation with regard to education, health and security, with a society organised under the precepts of law and ethics. If necessary, it will know how to repress, internally and externally, threats to its sovereignty, as well as the action of individuals and organisations that affront the rules of social coexistence, the rights of citizens and national institutions.

The firm, patriotic considerations of Ambassador Araújo de Castro, spoken in 1971, still reflect the direction of the Brazilian nation; in his words,

> no country escapes its fate and, fortunately or unfortunately, Brazil is condemned to greatness. Condemned to it for several reasons, due to its territorial extension, to its demographic mass, to its ethnic composition, to its socioeconomic system and to its irrepressible desire for progress and development. Either we accept our destiny as a great, free and generous country, without resentment and without prejudices or we run the risk of remaining on the sidelines of history, as a people and a nation.

INTRODUCTION

This book is a direct result of the lecture that I gave at the opening ceremony of the traditional Italian Week on the 1st June, 2013, at the invitation of the *Amici d'Italia* society, in São José do Rio Preto, São Paulo. The theme of the lecture, "The Campaign Of The Brazilian Expeditionary Force (FEB) to the Liberation of Italy," is dear to all Brazilians, Italian descendants or otherwise, due to the remarkable contribution that the action of Brazilian troops represented regarding the promotion of the rule of law, the observance of human rights and the prevalence of democratic order on a global scale.

This campaign also had considerable importance for the liberation of Italy from the forces of evil, which brought so much misfortune and suffering to its people. Finally, the feeling that inspired the Brazilian action had relevant domestic consequences, and helped to consolidate the still incipient democracy in the country.

The national day of Italy, the 2nd June, occurred the day after my talk. It was thus defined by the date of the plebiscite in 1946, in which the Italian people opted for the end of the monarchy and the establishment of the Italian Republic, and created the foundations for constitutional order and democracy in the country. According to General Mark Clark, commander of the Fifth Army of the United States of America, into which the FEB was integrated, "men of many nations lost their blood in Italy for the cause of freedom", including many Brazilian heroes.

As the son of an Italian mother (and a Brazilian father) and citizen of Brazil and Italy, I had the double satisfaction of addressing this issue, and I should also record the enormous pleasure of having had by my side, on the occasion, my uncle, Ruy de Noronha Goyos, 99 years of age at the time, who served with discipline, honour and distinction in the cause of our country and democratic freedoms as a member of the FEB in the theatre of war in Italy. He was a Sergeant of the 6th Engineer Battalion, which shipped out of Rio de Janeiro in June 1944. The numerous friends present at the time paid a tribute to Sergeant Ruy de Noronha Goyos which was both spontaneous and emotive.

I would also like to thank my dear friend, Rosalie Gallo y Sanches, president of *Amici d'Italia*, for her kind invitation to the conference in my beloved homeland, and also my dear friend, Adhemar Bahadian, former ambassador of Brazil to the Italian Republic, for the suggestion that I address this subject matter, as he was frustrated with the neglect of FEB's glorious deeds, not only in Italy but also – and mainly – in Brazil.

I would like to record the encouragement received from Professors Luiz Alberto Moniz Bandeira and Luis Antonio Paulino, who read the initial manuscript. I am also grateful to Brigadier Sérgio Xavier Ferolla, who wrote the foreword to this work with precious memories, and to Dr. Walter Sorrentino, who wrote the afterword, recalling fundamental values. I wanted an afterword because the inheritance FEB's campaign continues to mark Brazil's constitutional structure and reflects national aspirations in our time, in addition having contributed to formatting current international law and, likewise, affirm values dear to humanity.

Dr. Aurelio Guzzoni, my friend, classmate and former partner, read the original book and gave helpful comments for which I am also very grateful, as well as having provided testimony concerning the history of his family members in the resistance against Nazi fascism in the city of Bergamo, in the Lombardy region of Italy, which is mentioned in the work.

After the lecture at *Amici d'Italia*, I made a two week trip to Italy and was able to revisit the area where the theatre of operations of the FEB had been situated, which I had known for more than 25 years, and was also able to research some files on the resistance, as well as the writings of Antonio Gramsci and Palmiro Togliati concerning fascism, and others on Nazism.

The work was then expanded as a result of the notes I made at the time, including on the geography of the region where Brazilian troops operated, which is described in the report on FEB actions. I made the town of Levanto, in Liguria, my centre of operations, in the company of my daughter, Anita de Noronha Goyos, and my goddaughter, Georgia Daneri.

This book purposely transcends the military actions of Brazil in World War II because it seeks to contextualise the conflict in the economic, political and social developments that affected the world in the early twentieth century and that initially led to fascism in Italy and, later, to Nazism in Germany.

Thus, I sought to explain the underlying conditions for the development of fascism in Italy in the early 1920s, together with the spurious ideologies of the movement, its policy of internal repression and external imperial expansionism, all within a despairing economic, social and political framework, whilst paying particular attention to Mussolini's racist policy.

Likewise, the development of Nazism in Germany is examined from the end of World War I, in 1918. I examine the political conflicts of the time, the disbelief in democracy and the role of German nationalism arising from the creation of the nation state in 1870, in the creation of Nazi thought. I analyse Hitler's expansionist policy in international relations, together with the verified economic recovery and internal political repression in the domestic sphere, and again I discuss the issue of racism.

In Brazil, I discuss economic, social and political evolution from 1929 and their internal effects and examine the Revolution of 1930 and the various political developments that occurred in the 1930s and 1940s. Moreover, I report on aspects of foreign trade and the oscillating politics of President Getúlio Vargas and how the situation of the colonies of Italian (largest in the world), Japanese (largest in the world) and German immigrants (second largest in the world) presented itself in Brazil in that period.

I introduce the evolution of Brazilian foreign relations, highlighting the severance of relations with the Axis powers in early 1942, which led to the situation of belligerency with Germany and with Fascist Italy. I also report on the circumstances and the situation of risk, assessing the latter as an act of enormous political courage by the government of Getúlio Vargas, since it was implemented when the Axis powers were winning the war.

I introduce the coastal and South Atlantic war, the losses of Brazilian and allied ships, as well as their respective consequences for Brazil, and I examine the relevance of naval transport during this period. I also describe the situation of the Brazilian Navy and its formidable action in this episode, in protecting convoys and north-south transportation in Brazil. I examine the actuation of the Brazilian Air Force (*Força Aérea Brasileira*, FAB), created as an independent weapon in 1941, to combat the submarines of the Axis powers. I report on the understanding achieved between Roosevelt and Vargas, with respect to sending a Brazilian expeditionary force to the theatre of Italy operations. I discuss the formation of the FEB and the appointment of its commander, as well as the selection criteria of its ranks. I examine the formation of the Air Force Fighter Division of the FAB and the appointment of its commander. I disclose the extraordinary support received from national public opinion for the humanistic mission of the Brazilian armed forces, the burden of which was supported by the Brazilian nation, including full payment of armaments supplied by the United States under the Lend-Lease project.

I present the extraordinary actions of the Brazilian Army in the FEB, its strategic achievements, the liberation of Italian cities, the encirclement an entire German division following a pursuit of 130 miles (209 km), and its victims. I report on the heroic action of the FAB in the Italian theatre and discuss the disproportionately high results of their actions, together with the personal sacrifice of its officers.

In the epilogue, I evaluate the effects of World War II on international relations and in shaping international public law and the advancement in public ethics. I further examine the effects of the conflict on Brazil, Italy, Germany and Japan, as well as the excellent relations of the country with those other countries in the post-war period.

28 DURVAL DE NORONHA GOYOS JR.

Finally, I hope that this modest work will serve as a contribution to the maintenance of the important historical memory of Brazilian action in the liberation of Italy and in defence of the highest humanistic values, such that they are always preserved. Likewise, I trust that the book and the memories it elicits serve to further approximate Brazil and Italy in the bonds of brotherhood and friendship that are instilled not only by common ideals, but the strong sociological component imparted by Italian immigration in Brazil.

1
Fascist Italy

As a young man, in October 1969, Luiz Alberto Moniz Bandeira, who subsequently become the greatest Brazilian historian of all time, in the preface to the work of the great Brazilian jurist, Professor Alberto da Rocha Barros (1969), wrote that fascism, contrary to what many imagine, is not a phenomenon specific to Italy and Germany, which, at a particular time, threatened to spread throughout the world. It arises wherever and whenever financial capital is unable to maintain balance in society by the normal means of repression, dressed in the classical forms of legality. Naturally, according to the specific conditions of time and place, fascism assumes different characteristics and colours, but essentially remains a peculiar type of State, a system of acts of force and police terror, permanent counter-revolution. It is the regime of declared civil war that has been institutionalised.

Indeed, fascism was responsible for the creation of the neologisms "totalitarianism" and "totalitarian", with which its supporters described the absolute power of the State under the control of a resolute man, the *"Duce"*. The totalitarian dictator behaves like a foreign conqueror on his native soil. Thus, we understand that the objective of totalitarian regime is the absolute domination of the nation and its control through the widespread use of State violence against civil society.

Mussolini's disrespect and contempt for civil society and its various manifestations were not only extraordinary, but shameful. Regarding national sentiment, the *Duce* even affirmed that "public opinion is a whore who goes with the male who wins".[1] In turn, the Secretary of the Fascist Party, Giovanni Giurati, pontificated that "Peace is not justice. Only violence prevails" (Makin, 1935, p.229).

The acceptance of the absolute power of the dictator is well characterised by the *"balila"* oath, of fascist youth, which imposed, "in the name of God and Italy, I swear to carry out the orders of the *Duce* and to serve with all my strength, and, if necessary, with my blood, the cause of the fascist revolution" (Galeotti, 2001, p.20).[2] In turn, under item 9 of the Decalogue of the militia, it states, *"Mussolini ha sempre ragione"* [Mussolini is always right] (Ibid., p.21).

According to Eric Hobsbawm (2012, p.268), fascism not only denied Marx, but also Voltaire and John Stuart Mill, and equally rejected all the heritage of the Enlightenment in the same way it repudiated socialism and communism. Politically,

---

1 "L'opinione pubblica è una puttana che va con il maschio che vince". (Mussolini apud Innocenti, 2013, p.99).

2 With respect to the author's translations into Portuguese, whenever possible, the original citations in English were located and those in Italian were translated directly into English from the originals.

fascism presented itself as a contradiction to the democratic state of law and, in fact, according to Mussolini (Hibbert, 2008, p.47), "Freedom is not an end; it is a means. As a means, it must be controlled and dominated." Likewise, Hermann Goering, one of the Nazi grandees, designated Christian morality and the humanism of the Enlightenment as "those stupid, false and unhealthy ideals" (Golghagen, 1996, p.457).

Thus, Palmiro Togliati (1976, p.1) defined fascism as "a blatant terrorist dictatorship of the most reactionary, chauvinistic and imperialist elements of financial capital." Fascism truly represented the interests the extreme right, of the large companies and banks, aside from sponsoring extreme nationalism. Furthermore, Mussolini naturally sought to expand the imperialist and Italian colonial interests *manu militari*.

Mussolini took power through a coup, a march of approximately 25 thousand militiamen to Rome which led the king of Italy, Victor Emmanuel, to request that the *Duce* form a coalition government on the 28th October, 1922. Soon after, in 1925, the government, by now exclusively fascist, was granted extraordinary powers and the regime became an absolute dictatorship, with no opposition allowed and with institutionalised censorship.

At that time, Italy had about 45 million inhabitants, and its economy was still predominantly agricultural. The Italian industrial sector represented less than 33% of the Gross Domestic Product (GDP) and was concentrated in the north. The per capita income of southern inhabitants, an economically underdeveloped territory, was no more than 40% of that of residents in the north of the country.

Moreover, Italy had emerged victorious, but with 600 thousand dead, a million maimed and disabled, and its economy

32 DURVAL DE NORONHA GOYOS JR.

totally destroyed as a result of its participation in World War I. Its trade balance was negative and its balance of payments was achieved with difficulty with remittances from Italian emigrants dispersed all over the world. In the post-war period, there was massive unemployment, high inflation and economic depression.

Thus, the social upheaval resulting from the economic situation facilitated the rise to power of Benito Mussolini and his fascist movement.[3] In 1927, the Fascist government entered its corporatist phase, with widespread state intervention in the economic order and the banking and financial system. Dating from this year, the *Carta del Lavoro* [Charter of Labour], stated in its first article, that "the Italian nation [...] is a moral, political and economic unity, which is realised in full in the Fascist State." The situation of the country only worsened with the so-called Great World Depression, which began in 1929.

The cultural view of fascism was mediocre. According to Italian historian Giorgio Bocca (1996, p.67-68).

> history "without heroes", as a critical search for truth, of socioeconomic and political connections, is discouraged, the Middle Ages does not please, because it is "a dark age", the Renaissance pleases no less, because its mercantilist and supranational character appears heretical ... the only true and great love of fascism is that of Roman traditions that, erraticly, confuses monarchy, republic and empire, as well as the society of hard, strong habits with that of tyrannical luxury and cosmopolitanism.

---

3 According to Mussolini, "Fascism is not a party, it is a movement." *Il Popolo d'Italia*, 23rd of March, 1923.

To corroborate the previous assertion, as a young journalist and politician, Benito Mussolini himself had written that "in a man of state, the so-called 'culture' is, ultimately, an unnecessary luxury."[4]

In fact, Mussolini sought to promote Italian nationalism, in an exaggerated manner, to exalt certain historical and cultural values, randomly chosen for their value of mass psychology. Thus, while reviling it, he took advantage of legitimate efforts to promote the national character of Italy, which had only been unified in 1870, in the movement in which Giuseppe and Anita Garibaldi had stood out. The Italian dictator even prohibited the use of loanwords in the vernacular.

According to Lenin, the fascist ideology only emerged 'after the coup commanded by adventurous politicians', and was inspired by absurd themes, all of which bring down an entire universal conception of man and the world (1967, p.10). Lenin quotes Mussolini, in a text written in 1921, when the latter affirms that "Italian fascism has a need, under penalty of death, or worst, of suicide – to arm to itself with a doctrine body…" (Mussolini, 1921, p.10)

According Palmiro Togliati (2010, p.6), Gramsci saw fascism as "a new 'liberalism' under modern conditions" and victory of Mussolini as "an arbitrary solution of a conflict from a catastrophic perspective." Togliati complemented Gramsci's concept presenting fascism as "the dictatorship of the bourgeoisie."

However, the general crisis of the capitalist system in Italy was not interrupted by the fascist regime. According to Antonio Gramsci (apud Canfora, 2012, p.303-ss),

---

4 Benito Mussolini, "Imponete una disciplina!" *Il Popolo d'Italia*, 15th of Dec., 1919.

34   DURVAL DE NORONHA GOYOS JR.

under the fascist regime, the possibilities of existence of the Italian people have decreased. There was a reduction in the system of production [...] The industrial sector itself was only saved from complete collapse by reducing the standard of working classes, by increasing working hours, by inflation [...].

And the middle classes, who had placed all their hopes on the fascist regime, "were ensnared by the general crisis" (Ibid., p.209).

In 1935, 500 thousand men of the fascist armed forces invaded Ethiopia, one of two areas in Africa that had not succumbed to imperialism and, *inter alia* resorting to mustard gas, deposed Emperor Haile Selassie, with the support of the Catholic Church and at a cost of 20% of the annual budget of Italy. Impoverished, Ethiopia at that time, had 10 million inhabitants, still practiced slavery and its foreign trade was only 2 million pounds (Makin, ibid, p 229-ss). Its main import product, salt, represented 41% of its list of purchases.

The country's capital, Addis Ababa, was occupied on the 5th May, 1936. On this occasion, Mussolini declared that "Italy finally has its own empire. A fascist empire, an empire of peace, an empire of civilisation and humanity" (Bosworth, 2005, p.367). The harsh economic sanctions imposed by the League of Nations, under the initiative of the United Kingdom, were ridiculed by the Italian dictator, and the process of colonisation of Libya was then intensified by Fascist Italy.[5]

Mussolini cynically declared that the war in Abyssinia was waged to carry out the highest social justice for those Italians

---

5 During this period, Italian emigration to Brazil declined, since the fascist government favoured the colonisation of its African empire.

who fought for the most elementary conditions of life. However, the Italian Communist Party denounced that the big capitalists earned much from the war in Abyssinia, but the Italian people would pay the price for the war, the colonisation and the larger conflict that was approaching.[6]

In 1936, Mussolini pledged to collaborate with Franco in the Spanish Civil War and sent a contingent of eighty thousand soldiers to the Iberian Peninsula, in support of Spanish Fascism, against the Republican forces of the democratic government. Then, in 1939, Italian troops deposed King Zog of Albania, and established the Italian imperial order therein. Such actions naturally alienated Italy from the community of nations and had the added effect of approximating the country with the other villain in the international order: Nazi Germany.

The fascist totalitarian state could not accept any parallel power and so Mussolini decided to actively combat organised crime, particularly the Mafia, with prominent actuation in Sicily. For this purpose, he appointed a former mayor of Bologna, Cesare Mori, who undertook an organised military operation against the Mafia between 1925 and 1929, which naturally received the recognition of the Italian population. An advertising campaign highlighted the effective results of combating organised crime.

In 1937, Mussolini accepted an invitation from Hitler to visit Germany. In November of the same year, Italy signed a pact with Germany and Japan against international communism. In December of that year, Italy withdrew from the League of Na-

---

6 Manifesto del Partito Comunista Italiano, *Lo Stato Operaio*, Aug., 1936.

36   DURVAL DE NORONHA GOYOS JR.

tions, and in 1938, Hitler made an official state visit to Italy, and was delighted with the welcome.[7]

On the 22nd May 1939, Italy and Germany signed the so-called Pact of Steel, a diplomatic and military alliance with offensive and defensive characteristics. The future of Italy was sealed in the short-term! According to the treaty, if one country were to go to war, irrespectively of whether or not they were the aggressor, the other pledged to support it with all their military forces.

The treaty was a German initiative, signed perfunctorily by Mussolini and harshly criticised by his Minister for Foreign Affairs, Galeazzo Ciano,[8] "A treaty, in which one accepts without discussion, the text prepared by the other party, is never good" (Innocenti, 2013, p.47).

In reality, Mussolini feared being isolated in Europe in a conflict between Germany and the Western democracies. He had tried to negotiate a treaty of alliance with France and England, without success, and believed that the Pact of Steel would exert pressure against France and would allow Italy to put weight on Germany with the purpose of at least delaying a military confrontation. That was not the view his Minister of Foreign Affairs, who wrote that they were Nazi madmen sought war at all costs (Ibid., p.58).

On the other hand, Mussolini was far from being naive and knew of the potential difficulties of a defensive and offensive treaty with Nazi Germany. According to the *Duce* (Ibid.,

---

7 Crowds welcomed Hitler in Rome, Naples and Florence, according to Joseph Goebbels (1993, p.152-ss)

8 Son of Mussolini's son-in-law, a member of a noble family from Livorno in Tuscany, and representative of the high Italian economic interests.

p.73), "the Germans are terrible as enemies and unbearable as friends." According to Mussolini, "in international relations there is only one moral: success" (Farrell, 2003, p.313).

In the meantime, the economic difficulties in Italy worsened due to demographic pressure on the one hand, and the loss of potential revenues arising from the remittances of immigrants on the other, since emigration had been restricted due to the preferential option of military conscription and by the colonisation process.

One of the saddest pages of the fascist dictatorship in Italy concerns the racist policy of the State. In 1938, under the aegis of the Ministry of Popular Culture, a manifesto[9] was published which *inter alia* stated that:

- human races exist;
- there are greater and lesser races;
- the concept of race is purely biological;
- the population of Italy is mostly of Aryan origin and its civilisation is Aryan;
- there is an Italian race;
- the time has come for Italians to declare themselves racist;
- Jews do not belong to the Italian race.

The Catholic Church was officially opposed to the measures.

In 1939, the law[10] forbade marriage between Jews and Italians, vetoed the employment of Jews in financial institutions, newspapers and registries, and limited the role of Jews in the so-called intellectual professions. Furthermore, it the attendance

---

9 Magazine *La Difesa della Razza*, 5th of Aug., 1938.
10 Law 1.024, of the 13th of July, 1939.

38 DURVAL DE NORONHA GOYOS JR.

of Jews in Italian public schools was prohibited, and their right to property remained limited. Goebbels (1993, p.234) called racist Italian law a "triumphant success for us."[11] The Jewish population in Italy at that time was about fifty thousand people.

After the outbreak of the Second World War, the situation of Jews in Italy deteriorated sharply. According to Michele Sarfatti (2005, p.105-6), from December 1943 onward,

> the vast majority of Jews on the peninsula were imprisoned and then transferred to the field of national screening of the Italian police ... principally for deportation to the camp at Auschwitz-Birkenau.

In 1944, all remaining assets in the possession of Jews were transferred to the State.[12]

At this point, it must be mentioned that fascism never achieved Italian national consensus, although it had enjoyed an enthusiastic support of the majority of the population for many years. In Mussolini's rallies, important for his politics of the masses, many young Italian women carried their children in their arms, lifted them up and shouted hysterically, *"Duce,* our children belong to you."[13]

It is worthy, mentioning that important libertarian forces were always opposed to fascism and, if this was not expressed

---

11 For him, the law was against the Jews and against Africa and in favour of the Northern Aryan.

12 Legislative Decree XXII 2 of the 4th January 1944 (Sarfatti, op. cit., p.111).

13 "Duce, i nostri figli vi appartengono." As reported by Fabrizio Guzzoni his son, Aurelio, and forwarded to the author in his testimony on the 1st of August, 2013.

with greater vigour, it was due to the character of the brutal dictatorship imposed. The tenacious armed resistance movement is a striking example of this situation. However, civil resistance to fascism has always existed, from the onset of the spurious regime (Monti, 1951, p.111).

As an example of the reaction as to how the opposition made itself felt in civil society, is the case of the great Italian intellectual Benedetto Croce. Regarding him, Antonio Gramsci (1948, p.179) observed,

> while many intellectuals lost their heads and did not know how to position themselves in the widespread chaos, reneging their own past the past itself, they floated in search of whoever was the strongest, Croce remained undisturbed in his serenity and affirmation of his faith that, metaphysically, evil cannot prevail and history is rationality.

In the city of Bergamo in Lombardy, northern Italy, brothers Fabrizio and Vittorio Guzzoni, the sons of Hotelier Aurelio Guzzoni, from Albergo Moderno, joined the resistance in 1940. Identified early on, Fabrizio crossed the border and joined the French Resistance in 1941, where he was injured during actions. In turn, Vittorio Guzzoni continued clandestinely in Italy until the end of the war. When wounded, he was rescued by a family, where he met his future wife. In turn, Aurelio senior was arrested for publicly burning the fascist flag.[14]

---

14 According to personal testimony given by Aurelio Guzzoni, junior, to the author in 2013.

Mussolini in his prime.

2
NAZI GERMANY

The great English economist John Maynard Keynes (2002, p.99), commenting on the Treaty of Versailles in 1919, signed at the end of the First World War, which occurred between 1914 and 1918, stated that "apart from other aspects of the transaction, I believe that the campaign for securing out of Germany the general costs of the war was one of the most serious acts of political imprudence for which our statesmen have ever been responsible."

Indeed, Keynes continued (op. cit., p.158)

People will not always silently accept death through starvation: Some will be taken by lethargy and despair, but other temperaments will be inflamed, taken by the nervous instability of hysteria, which can destroy what remains of the social organisation, submerging civilization with attempts to satisfy individual needs. This is the danger against which all our resources and courage and idealism must now cooperate.

42   DURVAL DE NORONHA GOYOS JR.

Nobody foresaw the conditions for the rise of Nazism in Germany with such clarity, accuracy and perception as Keynes. Such an environment favoured the consolidation of the leadership of Adolf Hitler and the National Socialist German Workers' Party (Nazi Party), although no party program or ideology that could be presented to the German people. Rather, the action of the party was founded on the most scabrous demagoguery, the most vile prejudices and cynical and ineffectual promises.

In his main work, *Mein Kampf* (My Struggle), Adolf Hitler (2005, p.293) thus presents his worldview:

> The Nazi party appropriates the initial characteristics of the basic thoughts of a general racist conception of the world; and, taking into consideration the practical reality, the timing, the available human material, with its weaknesses, forms a political faith which, within the rigid organization of the masses, entails the forecast of the victory of this new doctrine.

What mattered to Hitler, more than a basic set of ideas put forward on a political platform, was the road to power, which showed his opportunism. As the British historian Ian Kershaw (1998, p.253) observed, the opponents of Hitler often underestimated the dynamism of Nazi ideas because of their diffuse character and the cynicism of its propaganda. Hitler had "a message of national redemption.

In a somber economic climate and social misery, anxiety, and division, permeated by perceptions of the failure and ineptitude of seemingly puny politicians, this appeal was powerful (Ibid., p.331).

The originality of this national redemption scenario concerned the role of Germany in the global order in contradiction to the imperialist, colonial economic system dominated by Britain and the United States. Hitler chose to make an epic challenge to this system and, for this purpose, mobilised the frustrations of the German people (Tooze, 2007 p.xxxiv). This challenge was a response to the crisis of the global capitalist system, which permitted the selective economic growth of a few.

Leon Trotsky, an intellectual exponent of the Russian Revolution and founder of the Red Army, commented with finely attuned perception that "National Socialism descends lower down: from economic materialism to zoological materialism. Nazism collected 'all the refuse of international political thought ... to make up the intellectual treasure of the new German Messianism'" (Deutscher, 1968 p.161).

In 1933, Germany suffered not only the economic consequences of the Treaty of Versailles, but the effects of the Great Depression that began in the United States America in 1929, including hyperinflation and mass unemployment. At that time, its population was about 65 million people.

In the period that followed World War I and the enactment of the Weimar Constitution, the national patriotic idea, or *völkisch*, was imposed on the nation and obtained a mass following. It did not take long for such ideas to consolidate into an organised movement: Nazism (Mosse, 2008, p.14).

It should be noted that, like Italy, Germany only became a National State in 1870 and, like the Italian peninsula, a great effort was made of affirming the cultural heritage and the national values. As with fascism, Nazism took advantage of the tendency to promote an exasperated nationalism. In this context, parliament came to be seen as source of national disunity, and the political class eventually lost credibility. As George Mosse

44 DURVAL DE NORONHA GOYOS JR.

observed (op. cit., p.20), "millions of Germans, mostly from the left, were never seduced by the ideology of Nazism, but millions were, and these prevailed."

The chaos resulting from the economic and social disorder was enough to motivate the Nazi hordes to demand in the streets and cabinets, using typical violence, the indication of Hitler as Prime Minister, a demand that was eventually fulfilled. In the following German parliamentary elections, held in March 1933, the Nazi Party won 43.9% of the vote, which assured them 288 of 647 seats in the Reichstag, the German parliament.

The election results led to full assumption of key posts in the government by members of the Nazi Party, then to some extent, a Keynesian economy was put in practice, with some degree of success. The systematic deconstruction of the democratic order was then initiated, with the repudiation of the restrictions imposed by the Versailles Treaty, the implementation of racist legislation and military expansionism.

Hitler's first minister of the economy, Hjalmar Schacht, directed state expenditures towards rearmament, devoting 10% of GDP for this purpose, and to the construction of public works, such as roads. To finance these expenditures so-called Mefo bonds were introduced.[1] With no foreign currency reserves

---

1 The acronym Mefo was formed by the initials of four major German business groups. Given the lack of credibility of the state regarding the launch of debt securities, Hjalmar Schacht worked it so that these groups launched publicly guaranteed private securities, and income obtained from these securities was used to finance public works. In other words, the ministries constructed the works and paid for the financing in time commensurate with the maturity of the debt. Thus, Schacht's scheme enabled private sector funding (at least in theory, because the guarantee for the Mefo securities was actually public), but it was the public sector that actually executed the works.

(Hitler, op. cit., p.9), Germany resorted to scriptural currency to compensate for barter transactions, and sought to substitute imports by domestic products.

This economic policy had the support of large German banking business groups, all reaping benefits from purchase orders and large public contracts. The four-year economic plan submitted by the Nazi government in 1933 contemplated an agrarian reform, social policies in the health area and retirement benefits, invest in public works, the substitution of imports, incentives for domestic industry, among other actions. In the same year, on the 8th June, without having had major problems with creditors, Germany declared a moratorium on foreign debt and allocated the corresponding resources to rearmament.

The economy began to grow fast, and German GDP increased 5.2% in 1934 and 6.2% in 1935 (Tooze, op. cit., p.63). As a result, the number of unemployed decreased dramatically, falling from about 6 million in 1933 to about four hundred thousand in 1939. Moreover, the real estate sector grew three-fold, and the automobile industry, greatly encouraged by the government, gained a huge boost.

On the other hand, the unions lost their liberty and strikes were banned the political parties were closed, and all and any opposition to the Nazi regime was prohibited, which culminated in dispatching politicians who opposed the government to concentration camps. Freedom of thought and expression was eliminated and censorship was applied to all sections of the press or expression.

Over thirty thousand book titles were banned and burned, among which books by the poet Heinrich Heine, who aptly observed that, "there where books are burnt, in the end human beings will be burnt" (Kershaw, op. cit., p.483). Among the authors banned and considered "degenerate literary expressions" by the Nazi regime were Franz Kafka, Stefan Zweig, Ernest Hemingway, Erich Maria Remarque, Sigmund Freud, Karl Marx and Karl Liebknecht.

Even jazz was banned, because the rhythm originated from inferior races, all according to a bizarre and preposterous law on degenerate art, sanctioned by Adolf Hitler in 1938 and proposed to him by Joseph Goebbels, the Nazi propaganda minister, who was also responsible for matters concerning culture.

Carl Schmitt, the main legal theorist of the Nazi regime, pointed out three basic principles that would govern the new constitutional and legal order: the State, the movement and the people. The State was driven by the movement, i.e. the *Führer*, the leader, while the people were the passive subject of the action of the former (Agamben, 2005). Schmitt, moreover, suppressed the concept of Man in the German Civil Code, replacing it with "Germanic blood" and "German honour", which became the basic principles of German law (Sherratt, 2013, p.101).

According to some disparate German legal experts, among the sources of German law stood the *Führer*'s plans (sic) (Barros op. cit., p.37). According to Schmitt, the *Führer* was not only the agent of the nation, but its highest magistrate and highest legislator (Sherratt, op. cit., p.102). That was the so-called *führerprinzip* (Leader Principle). The corporate state, *bündish*, repudiated the concept of equality between individuals and promoted a hierarchical system in which everyone had his/her place, from the slave to the conductor (Mosse, op. cit., p.422).

Racism was one of the repugnant pillars of Nazi ideology and responsible for one of the darkest pages of history, a theme extensively discussed by Hitler in his work (Hitler, op. cit., p.210-ss). Racism was based on spurious theories, part of the refuse that Trotsky referred to, by authors like Gobineau (1967), who wrote that the constitutive element of the Aryan nature was the aspiration for power and the conquest of inferior races.

The Englishman Houston Stewart Chamberlain, who repudiated *inter alia* racial miscegenation, was also a great inspirer of German racist thinking. In turn, Ludwig Woltmann understood that the German race had been preselected to dominate the earth (Mosse, op. cit., p.146-ss), leading the so-called strong and the decline of the weak.

The Aryan race was considered superior, whereas the remainder were seen as subhuman or monstrous. Persecution of the Jews became official State policy from 1933, with their exclusion from government jobs. In 1935, the so-called Nuremberg Laws were passed, which *inter alia* revoked the citizenship of German Jews. In 1936, 1937 and 1938, Jews were excluded from all regulated professions, such as law, journalism and medicine, and, from 1941 onwards, the German Jewish population was transferred to the infamous concentration and extermination camps in Eastern Europe. A program of physical elimination of the Jews and other segments perceived as enemies of the *Reich* was put into practice in 1942. However, besides Jews, other groups were also perceived as enemies: political opponents, most notably the communists, but also socialists, gypsies, freemasons, the clergy and homosexuals.

From 1936, this model began to subside and the German government directed their economic planning for war. In early 1938, Hitler promoted an uncontested invasion of Austria, promoting unification with Germany, or *Anschluss*, an action con-

48 DURVAL DE NORONHA GOYOS JR.

templated in *Mein Kampf*, as a "matter of life or death", which was achieved with no expressive resistance.

The Nazis began to put into practice the doctrine of expansion eastward, in search of the so-called vital territory (*lebensraum*), also the object of Hitler's work (op. cit., p.473-ss). This was the implementation of the Nazi vision of how to act in the face of British imperialism, founded in colonialism, for the purpose of economic gains. The Sudetenland, in Czechoslovakia, with an important minority population of Germans, was the object of Nazi greed and was integrated into the *Reich* in 1938, with the complacency of the English and French (Faber, 2008). This was followed by military occupation of the rest of the country and the creation of a "protectorate."

In 1939, Hitler decided to implement the plan to invade Poland in search of more vital territory to the German *Reich*. To achieve this, Nazi diplomacy, led by Joachim von Ribbentrop,[2] signed a nonaggression pact with the Union of Soviet Socialist Republics (USSR), represented by Vyacheslav Molotov, the Minister of Foreign Affairs, on the 24th August of that year.

The German Nazi and Italian Fascist diplomacy were conducted by two dilettantes who failed to formulate a consistent policy. Ribbentrop's background was that of a champagne salesman, and Ciano was Mussolini's son-in-law. The latter called Ribbentrop the "greatest of pigs" and a "war maniac", among other unedifying comments.[3] Meanwhile, Hitler was referring to Ciano as "that Viennese coffee dancer" (Innocenti, op. cit., p.131).

---

2 Later, Ribbentrop was sentenced to death by the Nuremberg Court and hanged.

3 Among other comments by Ciano, we can cite "fatuous, superficial, loquacious ..." (Ciano, 2005, p.195)

On the 1ˢᵗ September 1939, Nazi forces invaded Poland, and the treatment of the vanquished State was cruel. Hitler ordered "no mercy. Might makes right" (sic). Two days after the invasion, the United Kingdom and France declared war on Germany. World War II began in Europe.[4]

Between spring and summer of 1940, Germany occupied Denmark and France and defeated the British Expeditionary Force occupying Paris on the 14ᵗʰ June, having swept through Belgium, Luxembourg and the Netherlands. General Charles de Gaulle established a French government in exile, in London, and the predominance of the English navy in the Atlantic prevented Germany from being regularly stocked with raw materials necessary for the normal functioning of its economy, an episode that became known as the Battle of the Atlantic.

Previously, Germany had occupied Norway and established a regime sympathetic to the Nazis in the country.

Mussolini, imbued with a great sense of opportunism and taking only a border village, declared war on France and the United Kingdom after the defeat of the forces of these countries by Nazi troops (Mazower, 2008) in the French theatre of war.

Following a failed isolated attempt of an Italian invasion, originally with one hundred and sixty two thousand men and a heroic resistance, Greece surrendered to the Italo-German forces and was occupied in early 1941. The fascist Minister of War, General Pietro Badoglio,[5] had determined that all Greek cities

---

4 In Asia, the conflict began in 1937 with the Japanese invasion of Manchuria, in the northeast of the Republic of China.

5 Subsequent to the armistice, he was head of the Italian government. Accused by Ethiopia of war crimes in the campaign in that country due

50   DURVAL DE NORONHA GOYOS JR.

with more than ten thousand inhabitants were to be razed to the ground (Hastings, 2011, p.117). In that campaign, the Italian troops suffered casualties of about fifty thousand soldiers killed and one hundred fifty thousand wounded.

In turn, the United Kingdom was brutally attacked by the *Luftwaffe*, the German air force, in what is conventionally called the Battle of Britain,[6] in which military and industrial targets and British civilians were attacked, of whom one hundred and fifty six thousand died during this period. The British painstakingly prevailed in this conflict, while the outcome prevented the attempted invasion of the British Isles by the Nazis.

On year after the French surrender on the 22nd June 1941, Hitler unleashed Operation Barbarossa (Clark, 1995) and invaded the Soviet Union with one hundred and forty army divisions, obtaining an impressive success at first, occupying the western part of the country, arriving in Leningrad and a few miles short of Moscow. The initial battle front was 930 miles (1,500 km) long and expanded to 1,550 miles (2,500 km) before the end of that year. Mussolini had not had been informed in advance,[7] even so, he subsequently sent an unhappy expeditionary force of sixty thousand men to fight in Eastern Europe.

On the 7th December 1941, in response to an economic and financial boycott that had proved effective, Japanese forces at-

---

to the massive use of gas prohibited by the Vienna Convention of 1925, he was protected by the allies in the Cold War environment.

6 For the Battle of Britain, Fascist Italy sent about half its air force, which was technologically outdated compared with German and English equipment, leaving their troops in North Africa and the Mediterranean unguarded.

7 Mussolini (apud Farrel, op cit, p.350) criticised the invasion of the Soviet Union, calling it "cretinism and improvisation".

tacked the main United States base in the Pacific Ocean, Pearl Harbour, in Hawaii, devastating a large part of the north-American fleet. However, they did not destroy the aircraft carriers nor the two hundred airplanes of their embarked air force, thus bringing the Americans into the world conflict in conjunction with the Allies.

In January 1942, following a lightning campaign, one hundred thousand British and Australian soldiers and Indian colonial troops surrendered to the Japanese armed forces commanded by General Tomoyuki Yamashita,[8] in Singapore, a British colony, headquarters of the important and modern British naval base in South Asia.

Thus, the armed conflict spread, reaching an unprecedented global scale.

---

8 Sentenced to death by the Tokyo Tribunal, following the surrender of Japan.

Hitler takes Paris.

3
Aspects of Brazil in the late 1930s and the early 1940s

On the 30th October 1930, Washington Luís, then president of the Republic in Brazil, was deposed by an armed movement that was corporatist in nature, called the '*Tenentista*' revolt. Inspired to some extent by positivist philosophy, according to Nelson Werneck Sodré (1969, p.318), the *tenentismo* was "superficial [...] and modest in its aims. It began by assuming that everything depended on the men who were in power and that simply replacing them would lead to significant results."

The country, which at the time had approximately thirty seven million inhabitants, was undergoing a severe economic and social crisis resulting from the consequences of the collapse of the international financial markets of 1929. Exports of the main Brazilian product, coffee, fell dramatically and there was a substantial deficit in the balance of payments. The ruling classes, previously united, had broken apart, and politicians outside the traditional axis of power, located in São Paulo and

54   DURVAL DE NORONHA GOYOS JR.

Minas Gerais, especially those from Rio Grande do Sul, united for another military uprising (Ibid., p.320).

On the 3rd November 1930, Getúlio Vargas, leader of the movement and former finance minister of Washington Luís, entered Rio de Janeiro – the federal capital at that time – at the head of the revolutionary troops commanded by General Góis Monteiro. On the occasion, Vargas said he was "provisionally assuming Government of the Republic, as delegate of the Revolution, on behalf of the Army, the Navy and the People" (Basbaum, 1976 p.14). Interventionists, almost all lieutenants, were then appointed to govern the Brazilian federal states.

According to Leoncio Basbaum (Ibid., p.19-20), Vargas was very interested in the support of the lieutenants and made many concessions to them because

with or without the uniform, they represented two large forces togather: the military and the demagogic. Militarily, they dominated the army, due to their proximity to the troops, and could at any time rouse them. The lieutenants wanted fascism, strong government and a life and death struggle against communism and the revolutionary pretensions of the masses.

The so-call Constitutionalist Revolution in São Paulo, launched on the 9th July 1932, sought the resumption of power by the leaders of the Paulista Republican Party (PRP), which had been ousted by Getúlio Vargas. The Paulistas adopted the constitutionalist flag that reflected a national yearning, which was not only tempered, but also shaped by the deep economic crisis and the political and administrative excesses of the dictatorship.

Having beaten Paulista rebellion and with the resulting political prestige acquired, Vargas could hold elections, conducted in May 1933, in which, based on new voter registration and supervision of Electoral Justice, for the first time women and those aged above 18 years had the right to vote (Bourne, 2012, p.100-ss). The Constitution of 1934 had a bourgeois and, to some extent, liberal profile, with important influences of marked fascist character.

The new constitution contemplated the indirect election of the President of the Republic, which occurred on the 17th July 1934 – which unsurprisingly befell to Getúlio Vargas, with a mandate until 1938 – created classist representatives, as well as ratifyed all the acts of the dictatorial regime. Its effects were duly suspended in 1935 due to the state of siege then decreed, which lasted until the enactment of the Estado Novo, in 1937.

In 1935, Brazil signed preferential free trade agreements with the United States and Germany, obtaining advantages from both, which was a reflection of Getúlio Vargas' ambivalent policies. For example, Brazilian cotton competed in Germany with North-American cotton and, by virtue of the trade agreement, had preferential access at 24% lower cost. On the other hand, the traditional British economic influence in Brazil declined.[1]

During that period, Brazil was Germany's largest trading partner outside Europe. In turn, the United States of America was Brazil's largest trading partner. Since Brazil accumulated a enormous favourable trade balance in German scriptural currency the country was led to direct many of its purchases from Germany, if only for monetary compensation.

---

1 In the mid-1930s, the United Kingdom held 48% of the stock of direct foreign investments in Brazil.

56   DURVAL DE NORONHA GOYOS JR.

This situation, coupled with the refusal of the United States to sell weapons to Brazil, led the government of President Getúlio Vargas to resort to suppliers in the German market to modernise its military hardware. The same was true, but in a more limited manner, with regard to Italy.

According to reports from the U.S. ambassador to Brazil, Jefferson Caffery, to the Secretary of the American State Department, Vargas' foreign policy consisted of extracting the maximum from the United States, on the one hand, and the maximum from the fascist powers on the other.[2] Vargas' posture was, to some extent, premeditated, but it also reflected the ambiguities of the game of internal power in Brazil and the diversity of economic, social and political interests.

On the morning of the 10th November 1937, Vargas launched a putsch, a self-coup, and dissolved Congress by police action, avoiding the ostensive presence of the Army (Faust, 2006, p.80-ss). At 10:00 am the next day, the new constitutional charter was signed, drafted mostly by Francisco Campos, a man with strong fascist leanings. Vargas took all the power for himself, ruling by Decree (Burns, 1993, p.356-ss).

As Basbaum observed (op. cit., p.105), "the new Constitution dispensed with [...] Congress, the representative system, conforming to the fascist dictatorial system that concentrate in one hand the legislative and executive powers and, as became clear later, the Security Court and the Judiciary as well".

In December 1937, the political parties were closed down and censorship was institutionalised. Heráclito Fontoura Sobral Pinto, the renowned Brazilian jurist and a resident of the

---

2 Jefferson Caffery to Cordell Hull, Rio 22nd of April, 1939, 832.00/1255, RG59. Washington, USA: National Archives.

federal capital, defined the Constitution of 1937 as nothing less than "Nazi and fascist" (Dulles, 2001, p.311), and fervently opposed it.

Thus the Estado Novo was created, a designation borrowed from the bloodthirsty dictator Antonio Salazar of melancholy Portugal and which, according to Thomas E. Skidmore (1985, p.52), "represented a soften Brazilian version of the European fascist method." Unlike European fascism, Vargas did not rely on any fascist party in particular and did not pursue a racist policy, which would not only be insane, but also very difficult to implement in a multiracial country like Brazil.

Vargas explained the issue of rights and individual freedoms constitution in the 1937, as such:

> the Estado Novo does not recognise the rights of individuals against the society. Individuals have no rights, they have duties! The rights belong to the society! The state, superimposing itself on the struggle of interests, guarantees the rights of the society and enforces the fulfilment of duties towards it. (Fausto, op. cit., p.82)

The Estado Novo

in the ascension phase of fascism, took from the former its saddest ostensive form. However, if Italian fascism and German Nazism corresponded to a fully developed capitalist stage, the Estado Novo should correspond to an initial capitalist stage. The contradictions from which the Estado Novo emerged, and those that were maintained or appeared under it, presented a complexity that the police apparatus, repressive brutality and extreme centralisation could only disguise. (Sodré, op. cit., p.329)

58   DURVAL DE NORONHA GOYOS JR.

During the 1930s, the two major parties of the masses in Brazil were the *Partido Comunista Brasileiro* (PCB, Brazilian Communist Party), which presented itself to the nation as the *Aliança Nacional Libertadora* (ALN, National Liberation Alliance), outlawed in 1935, and *Ação Integralista* (AI, Integralist Action). The leader of the PCB was Luiz Carlos Prestes, whose life story was celebrated by Jorge Amado in *O cavaleiro da esperança* [The Knight of Hope] (1987), written in 1942. Prestes' wife, the German Olga Benário Prestes, eight months pregnant, was deported by Getúlio Vargas to Nazi Germany and interned in a concentration camp, where she eventually died.

Among the parties closed down in December 1937, due to their affinity with the Estado Novo, was *Ação Integralista*, led by Plinio Salgado. AI was the fascist-inspired Brazilian party, and numerous members were close to or even composed the Vargas government. Among the leading elements of AI was Miguel Reale,[3] "one of its more radical elements" (Seitenfus, 2003, p.51).

According to Sá Motta (2008, p.60), "integralism possessed a doctrine similar to facism." Its newspapers frequently praised Mussolini and Hitler, "even though the integralists liked to stress that their movement was nationalist, authentically Brazilian and inspired by national culture." Instead of black or brown shirts, they wore green.

In 1937, the fascist foreign minister, Galeazzo Ciano, decided to financially support *Ação Integralista* (Hart, 1991, p.139), before Getúlio Vargas' putsch, because of the existing ideological identities, and because the party's candidate for the presi-

---

3 Subsequently, Dean of the University of São Paulo during the Brazilian military dictatorship (1964-1986).

dential elections scheduled for that year (later frustrated), Plinio Salgado, was one of the favourites.

Dissatisfied with the closure of the parties, *Ação Integralista* attempted a failed coup, assaulting the Guanabara Palace in May 1938. The principal leaders of the integralist revolt had their flight to Italy organised by the Italian Ambassador, Vincenzo Lojacono, who forged the necessary documentation. Miguel Reale "left clandestinely on the 2nd July 1938, on the Italian ship Augustus bound for Genoa, under the false identity of Giovanni Sbraglia, an Italian citizen" (Seitenfus, op. cit., p.139).

The Constitution of 1937 had taken into account the risks of actions of foreign states against the sovereignty of Brazil. Indeed, Article 122 treated *inter alia* an attempt of submission of the national territory to the sovereignty of a foreign state as a crime subject to the death penalty. In this period, because of German racial laws, the pressure of immigration of Jewish refugees, among others, was enormous. Like all countries at this time the Brazilian government took measures to limit the number of such immigrants, but despite this, thousands entered the country during this period, usually as tourists, initially exceeding the period of stay, then later acquiring property in the country for the purpose of remaining.

The Brazilian government knew of the illegal procedures adopted, which were tolerated. Indeed, according to documents of the Brazilian Foreign Ministry, between 1933 and 1939, 65,189 Jews entered the country, the majority illegally, quite an expressive number (Neto, 2013, p.362-363). Moreover, it is worth noting that an insignificant number of Jews were expelled from Brazil (Ribeiro, 2010, p.476). In 1936, when the persecution of the Jews in Germany aggravated, Getulio Vargas allowed the German-Jewish community to inaugurate the Paulista Israeli

60 DURVAL DE NORONHA GOYOS JR.

Congregation (CIP), which was founded by the Major Rabbi Dr. Fritz Pinkuss, who was born near Magdeburg (Brazil-German Chamber, 2001, p. 114).

The governments of Germany and Italy decided to work with the Estado Novo, acclaimed in these countries. Both countries had large numbers of citizens in Brazil, who arrived from the second half of the nineteenth century onwards, as agricultural workers, particularly for the coffee plantations in the interior of the state of São Paulo. Between 1886 and 1914, Italian immigrants represented 44% of the total number of foreigners that entered Brazil (Trento, 200, p. 26). According to private estimates, in 1940, the Italian colony was about 3 to 5 million people. This contingent represented approximately 12% of Brazil's population during this period, half of whom resided in the state of São Paulo, which at the time already had the most developed economy in the country. According to figures of the Italian embassy in Brazil, the Italian community in São Paulo was, and remains to this day, "the largest in the world."[4]

The state of São Paulo alone had approximately 360 newspapers in Italian (Hart, op. cit., p.61), Rio de Janeiro had 64, and Rio Grande do Sul, 53. Brazil had about 400 Italian schools at this time, thanks to the initiative of immigrants and their descendants and religious orders and not the Italian and/or Brazilian governments. This number was more than twice that of Italian schools in Argentina and the United States combined. The Italian hospital in the City of São Paulo was Umberto I and half of the existing credit establishments were of Italian origin.[5]

---

4 Ambasciata d'Italia, "*Presenza Italiana in Brasile – Cenni sulle collettività*" [*The Italian presence in Brazil – Notes on the community*], Istituto Italiano di Cultura di San Paolo, 1999, p.34.

5 Ambasciata d'Italia, "Presenza Italiana in Brasile - Cenni sulle collettività", op. cit., p.47.

THE CAMPAIGN OF THE BRAZILIAN EXPEDITIONARY FORCE... 61

The main newspaper of the colony in São Paulo was the *Fanfulla*, a daily journal published in Italian language with about fifty thousand subscribers. In virtue of its propaganda value, direct control of this publication shifted to the fascist Italian government in 1934 and became the disseminator of its aberrant ideology. In 1942, publication of the newspaper was interrupted.

The fascist Italian government had some popularity with sectors of the Italo-Brazilian community principally due to its nationalist character. The truth is that, "besides the immediate compliance of the elite, it would be wrong to state that the Italian mass in Brazil identified ideologically with fascism" (2000, p.116). In any event, "the positive image of Mussolini and Italian fascism in Brazil only documents opinion in 1938 on the occasion of Italy's approximation with Germany (Rome-Berlin Axis)" (Carneiro, op. cit., p.450) and enactment of racist legislation by the Italian government.

In like manner, the German colony in Brazil in 1940 was estimated at between seven and nine hundred thousand people (Seitenfus, op. cit., p.11). There were 937 German schools in Rio Grande do Sul in 1930, and the population of German origin was also large in Santa Catarina, Paraná and São Paulo. The German hospital in São Paulo, founded in 1897, was the Humboldt, currently known as the Oswaldo Cruz German Hospital.

The German press also propagated. The newspaper *Deutsche Zeitung* reached the impressive run of fifty thousand copies daily in 1928 (Ibid., p.15). In April 1939, all foreign newspapers were closed, and in August, public use of foreign languages was banned, including in religious sermons.[6]

---

6 Decree-Law 1,545 of the 25th of August, 1939, which ruled on adaptation to the national setting by Brazilian foreign descendants.

62 DURVAL DE NORONHA GOYOS JR.

In November of the same year, education was nationalised in Brazil (Cervo, op. cit., p.149-ss). Political action by any foreign group or party in Brazil had been banned[7] in 1938, including the National Socialist German Workers' Party (NSDAP), a Brazilian section of the Nazi Party.

The Nazis sought to "re-germanize" the population in Brazil with German origin. In spite of the efforts made during the 1930's, which included many institutions and publications connected directly to the Nazi Party, such as Teuto-brasileira Youth Circle's , the German Women Union, Labor German Front and the *Volk und Heimat* almanac (Seyferth, 1999, p.295), the majority of Brazilians with German origins were seduced by the spurious ideology. In fact, "the resistence to the nazi advances also came from German-Brazilians"(Seyferth, op. cit., p.306).

Similarly, in 1940 the number of Japanese immigrants and their descendants was estimated at about six hundred and fifty thousand people, most of them living in the state of São Paulo, including 234,636 original immigrants[8] and the remainder, their descendants. Japanese immigrants and their descendants had 294 Nipponese schools[9] in São Paulo alone, dozens of newspapers and a hospital, Nippon Byoin, the Japanese Hospital.

Just between 1924 and 1941, 137.572 Japanese immigrants entered Brazil, recruited by the Japan Government through an State Company, a Kaigai Kogyo Kabushiki Kaisha (KKKK), which had as an objective the acquisition of properties for im-

---

7 Decree-Law 383 of April 18, 1938.
8 Celia Sakurai, "Imigração Japonesa para o Brasil. Um exemplo de imigração tutelada – 1908-1941". [*Japanese Immigration to Brazil. An example of tutored immigration – 1908-1941*]. Available at: www.clacso.org.ar/biblioteca.
9 História da Imigração, parte 3 [*History of the Immigration, part 3*] Available at: www.imigracaojaponesa.com.br.

migrant activities, as well as the managing of colonies in the country (Sakurai, op. cit., p. 16 – ss).

The many Japanese newspapers represented a means of disseminating, in the Japanese language, news concerning Brazil and world, besides providing a means of communication between the various oriental colonies located within the state of São Paulo. The main journal was the *Nippak Shimbun* daily, closed in 1941 and reopened in 1949, and which still exists today. According to Rogério Dezem (2010, p.244), "suspension of Japanese immigration to Brazil only took place in 1941, when the last group officially arrived on the ship Buenos Aires Maru", officially ending an era. The situation was extremely delicate, for most Japanese immigrants had been organized in Brazil by the Japanese Government itself.

By 1941, the combined number of citizens originating from Axis countries in Brazil was approximately 6.5 million people, almost 16% of the total population, and in this period, it was already possible to observe the process of racial miscegenation, a typical and happy Brazilian phenomenon, particularly with members of the Italian community.

Brazil's economic and financial situation deteriorated substantially, since the deficit of the balance of payments grew due to the dramatic fall of the balance of trade, a consequence of the fall in international prices of agricultural commodities. It was then, in 1938, that Getulio Vargas declared a unilateral moratorium on foreign debt, which meant that Brazil lost access to the voluntary international financial markets.

In Brazil, there was fear of a potential German initiative to induce the separation of the three southern states of the country, with the purpose of creating the so-called Antarctic Germany, due to the high concentration of the population of German origin in that area of the national territory, comprising the states of

Rio Grande do Sul, Santa Catarina and Paraná, and due to the action of philo-Nazi parties.

Such fears were not unfounded, since Hitler had already declared that he had special interests in Brazil. "We shall build a new Germany in Brazil. There, we'll have what we need" (Rauschning, 1940, p.63). The German dictator believed Brazil was in perfect conditions to start "a revolution capable of transforming, in a few years, a State governed by corrupt mestizos into a Germanic Domain". Hitler proposed to send capital and entrepreneurial spirits to Brazil, as well as his political ideas. "If there is one continent where democracy is an absurdity and a means to suicide, it is South America" (Rauschning, op. cit., p. 64).

With the outbreak of the European phase of World War II, on the 1st September 1939, Brazil gradually distanced itself from the Axis countries, more ideologically related to the Estado Novo regime, and approached the United States, which openly supported France and England in the conflict. This choice was made for economic and financial reasons, since the United States was Brazil's largest trading partner at the time. Moreover, any Brazilian exports to Germany and Italy were subject to the British naval blockade.

On the other hand, the deficit in the balance of payments and loss of access to voluntary international financial markets of credit under the moratorium led Brazil, forcibly, to a policy of import substitution, which represented a substantial increase of the light industry in the country. Furthermore, there was an increase direct state intervention in railways, navigation and basic industries, such as oil and steel, (Skidmore, op. cit., p.76).

United States diplomacy, anticipating the country's entry in the world conflict and the need to cooperate with Brazil in the supply of strategic products and to facilitate bases in the South Atlantic, approached the Vargas government, a move that was

THE CAMPAIGN OF THE BRAZILIAN EXPEDITIONARY FORCE... 65

heavily criticised in the American media because of Brazil's undisguised fascist bias. In 1940, the United States offered Brazil a line of credit from the US Eximbank, thereby funding for the industrial sector.

From June 1940 onwards, Brazil began to negotiate an eventual military cooperation with the Americans, in the event that the global armed conflict spread to the continent. In this eventuality, the Americans wanted access to facilities and guarantees of protection of the regions Rio de Janeiro, Salvador, Natal, Fortaleza, Sao Luis, Teresina, Recife and Belem (Seitenfus, op. cit., p.247), because they feared both an armed incursion by the Axis in the region and separatist movements involving Axis citizens in Brazil. Vargas, however, was still reluctant and sought to carry out a policy of equilibrium that would allow him to take advantage of the contradictions between the various imperialist powers. The Americans viewed Vargas' position with suspicion, and the converse was equally true.

However, from May 1941, Vargas adopted a posture of compliance with the United States on the issue of continental defence and instructed the Brazilian diplomacy to seek the support of other Latin American countries, holding a Pan-American Conference to this end, in June of that year, in Rio de Janeiro.

On such occasion, the Brazilian Foreign Minister, Oswaldo Aranha, an old friend and colleague of Vargas from Law School in Porto Alegre, warned the Brazilian dictator concerning Argentina's proclaimed intention of neutrality, speaking with great realism, in the sense that Brazil depended more on the United States (four fifths of coffee exported, loans) than the country of *La Plata Basin* (Hart, op. cit., p.167). At the same time, President Getúlio Vargas realised that "under normal peacetime conditions, Brazil would not have a margin of privileged negotiations" (Neto, op. cit., p.386) with the United States and pursued the strategic goal of installing a steel mill in the country, having obtained a grant from Eximbank in the amount of US$45 million, a sum that represented half the total cost of Volta Redonda.

One day after the Japanese attack on Pearl Harbour, the Vargas government declared solidarity with the United States; in turn, on the 11th December 1941, Germany and Italy declared war on the American country. On the 28th January 1942, at the end of a meeting of continental foreign ministers, held in Rio de Janeiro, most of the participating States agreed to sever relations with the Axis, with the exception of Argentina and Chile (Sander, 2007, p.31). On that very date, Brazil broke relations with the Axis countries and Germany immediately declared a state of belligerence against Brazil.

On the occasion, Oswaldo Aranha said, with an honesty that was very rare in a diplomat, that "it was not Getúlio, nor I, nor anyone that forced us to sever relations. It was our geographic position, our economy, our history, our culture, in short, the condition of our lives and the need seek to survival" (Hilton, 1994, p.389). Joseph Goebbels, on the other hand, believed Osvaldo Aranha to be "someone bought by Roosevelt"(Goebbels, 1942-1943, p. 140).

Following the same spirit and line of thought of Joseph Goebbels, Berlin Radio which was subordinated to the Minister, asked, in their transmissions for Latin America, "could there be a more undeniable proof that Brazil has become a colony, a protectorate of North America?" (sic) (Neto, op. cit., p.419).

On the 14th August 1941, Franklin Roosevelt and Winston Churchill signed the Atlantic Charter (Plesch, 2011, p.24-5), with principles that should govern the global legal order in the post-war period. In the Atlantic Charter, Article 5 proposed the development of international law in several sectors. In turn, Articles 2 and 3 dealt with the self-determination of nations, subject that countered British imperialist interests and which was reluctantly accepted by them, by virtue of pressure from the North-Americans. Article 4 also represented a tough setback to British imperialist interests[10] by promoting the germ of the most favoured nation clause, which would later be the basic principle of the General Agreement on Tariffs and Trade, 1947 (Goyos Junior; Noronha, 1995, p.11-ss).

On the 3rd March 1942, the United States ratified a Lend-Lease agreement with Brazil, which contemplated the supply of arms and munitions of war of two hundred million dollars,[11] an expressive value for the time, with a reduction of 65% of its true value and under favourable credit conditions (Seitenfus, op. cit., p.280). Next, agreements were reached that permitted the presence of American troops in the northeastern region of Brazil and a Joint Military Technical Commission was created, with representatives from both countries.

At that time, the Brazilian Army had a contingent of approximately 66,000 soldiers organised into five infantry divisions, three of which were transferred to the northeast, under the command of General Leitão de Carvalho (Campbell, 1992, p.5). The rest of the troops would remain, as usual, on the country's border with Argentina, which was then perceived not only as a regional rival, but as Brazil's principal potential foreign enemy.

In like manner, the *Força Aérea Brasileira* (FAB, Brazilian Air Force), an independent weapon since 1941, managed to be

---

10 Churchill only accepted the non-discriminatory principle in international trade as "the price to be paid for the Lend-Lease programme" (Steil, 2013, p.14).

11 Subsequently, the value amounted to three hundred and sixty million dollars, paid in full by Brazil in instalments, the last of them settled on the 1st July 1954. For a more in-depth reading, see "Causas e consequências da participação do Brasil na II Grande Guerra" [*Causes and consequences of Brazil's participation in World War II*], published by the Brazilian National Press Department in 1958, in Rio de Janeiro.

68   DURVAL DE NORONHA GOYOS JR.

more ill-equipped than the Army, possessing about 200 aircraft, few of which were for combat and none were modern. However, Brazilian pilots had important practical experience resulting from the national airmail service, particularly in the area of navigation. Either way, the FAB transferred contingents equipped with material capable of performing maritime reconnaissance to bases located in the northeast of the country, under the command of Air Commodore Eduardo Gomes (Ibid., p.6).

Air bases were established in Amapá, Belem, São Luís, Fortaleza, Natal, Recife, Maceió, Salvador and Caravelas, all of which of utmost importance to military aviation operations. These were related to the protection of the flows of maritime navigation, both domestic and international, as well as the antisubmarine campaign along the extensive Brazilian coastline.[12] Without the Natal airbase, in particular, Allied efforts in North Africa would have faced insurmountable logistical problems.

In contrast to the situation of the Army and the FAB, the Brazilian Navy was much better off, because the rearmament program was progressing well. This had much to do with the traditional Brazilian capacity for naval construction established in national territory.

In 1937, Brazil had received three new Italian-built submarines,[13] which were added to another, built in 1929, also from Italy. By way of comparison, in 1938, Italy had 70 submarines (Goebbels, 1993, p.144), while the Germany Navy had over a

---

12 Incaer (Instituto Histórico-Cultural da Aeronáutica), "A participação da Força Aérea Brasileira na II Guerra Mundial" [*Participation the Brazilian Air Force in World War II*]. Available at: www.incaer.aer.mil.br.

13 Tamoio, Tupi and Timbira, of the Italian Perla class, were submarines for coastal use. Some units of this class served in the Phalanx Navy during the Spanish Civil War. During World War II, submarines of this class served in the Mediterranean, with some success.

thousand submarines during the course of World War II (Werner, 1969, p.xxi).

However, the few Brazilian submarines could not be used in the military operations that followed, restricting their use to training the cadres of the Brazilian Navy, to avoid the risk of being confused with those of the Fascist Italian regime (Campbell, op. cit., p.15). This provides us with a strong historical lesson of yet another motive for not acquiring weapons from potential enemies or unreliable sources, for whatever reason.

The Brazilian fleet also had nine modern destroyers of English and American design, launched between 1940 and 1941, and other smaller ships. The flagship of the Brazilian fleet was the battleship Minas Gerais, which was similar to thebattleship São Paulo, both constructed around 1910, though the former had been modernised in 1939 (Ibid., p.7). In September 1941, Brazil offered the use of the Recife and Salvador bases to the South Atlantic Force of the U.S. Navy, then commanded by Admiral Jonas Ingram.

The Brazilian Navy had begun to train Brazilian merchant ships to travel in convoy, using Carioca class vessels as escort (Ibid., p.8). It is noteworthy that, in the early 1940s, the transport of cargo and passengers between southern and northern/northeastern Brazil was still done by sea, just like in the days of the Empire. Thus, the proper functioning of Brazilian maritime transportation was not only of vital importance, but a key strategic issue, since it was not only foreign trade that was at risk, but also domestic trade and communications.

President Getúlio Vargas.

Chancellor Osvaldo Aranha.

4
THE COASTAL DEFENCE OF BRAZIL AND MARITIME AND AERIAL WAR IN THE SOUTH ATLANTIC

With the mere threat of belligerence coming from the German Embassy following the severance of diplomatic relations between Brazil and the Axis countries on the 28th January 1942, chiefly Germany, but also Italy, initiated a maritime war against the means of Brazilian naval transportation, taking care to avoid attacks on the country's ports. Brazil's long coast, measuring 4,600 miles (7,400 km) in length, is very difficult to protect even today.

Military mobilisation and the defence of Brazil's coastline was concentrated on the northeastern region of the country, due to its geographic situation,[1] because it represents a continental salient protruding into the South Atlantic facing North Africa, and also due to German access to the western coast of Africa

---

1 For further information, access: www.exercito.gov.br/web/guest/na-ii-guerra-mundial.

74 DURVAL DE NORONHA GOYOS JR.

through the French colonies. The Allies feared an attempt of a German continental invasion from this sector.

Given the risks of transportation and the state of belligerence, a supply crisis occurred in the country, including essential items such as fuel, bringing with it an increase in prices and inflation. In May 1942, the freighter Commander Lyra was torpedoed in Cape São Roque by an Italian submarine, the Barbarigo, which was subsequently attacked by a Brazilian Air Force B-25 Mitchell bomber with the launch of eight bombs (Ferraz, n.d., p.39-40).

In early June 1942, three Brazilian merchant navy freighter vessels, or of mixed function, which included the ships Alegrete and Paracuri, were sunk by German and Italian submarines along the Brazilian coast, with heavy loss of life.

In July, the ships Tamandaré, Barbacena and Piave were sunk. Between the 18th and 19th August 1942, five Brazilian freighters were sunk by the German submarine U-507, the Ararát, Baependi, Aníbal Benévolo, Itagiba and Araraquara, totalling approximately 650 deaths including crew and passengers.

Great indignation and commotion was felt in national public opinion. In an improvised speech, inconsistent with his habits, Getúlio Vargas declared in Rio de Janeiro, "all of you return to your homes, with a clear conscience and head held high. The events that have been registered in the past few days will not affect the heart of Brazil, because, above all, Brazil is immortal. Long live Brazil" (Neto, op. cit., p.422).

For the 4th July 1942, the national day of the United States, the glorious National Union of Students (UNE) convened a demonstration of solidarity in front of the American embassy. Sectors of Vargas government represented by the Chief of Police in Rio de Janeiro, Filinto Müller, roused themselves to prevent the act, which actually occurred without incident and showed large, spontaneous popular support (Seitenfus, op. cit., p.298). Similar demonstrations occurred throughout the country.

The great Brazilian jurist, Sobral Pinto, who was already 49 years-old at the time, stated that "the day they enact general enlistment in the country, I shall present myself to the military authorities, like any other citizen, to provide whatever service I can" (Dulle, op. cit., p.219).

On the 22nd August 1942, Brazil officially recognised the state of belligerency and finally declared war on Germany and Italy on the 31st August. As Ruy and Buonicore well observed (2010, p.75), "the long delay between the beginning of torpedoing of our ships and the decreeing of war shows the vacillations that still existed within the government." However, the declaration of war against the Japanese Empire was only made in June 1945, i.e. less than two months before the end of the military conflict against the Japanese forces. Thus, Seintenfus (op. cit., p.300) aptly observes

beginning with Brazils entry into the war, the situation of the Vargas' government, particularly that of the president-dictator, becomes uncomfortable. Vargas officially fights against the Axis for freedom and democracy, while at the same time maintaining the country under a dictatorial regime, a pale copy of the European dictatorships.

Brazil's declaration of war against the Axis powers was much more significant and courageous because it occurred at a time in which the Nazi and fascist forces prevailed in the conflict, occupying almost the entire European continent. The decisive turn in World War II in favour of the Allies would occur only around the 31st January 1943, when the Axis forces in that theatre of operations surrendered to Red Army troops following the Battle of Stalingrad on the Eastern Front.[2]

On the 8th November 1942, Allied forces commanded by U.S. General George S. Patton landed in Morocco and Algeria, and fought the Axis armies, who counted on 1 million Italian men in Libya, plus the German forces of Field Marshal Erwin Rommel, the *Afrika Korps*. The Axis armies surrendered on the 12th May 1943, in the North African theatre of war.

With the declaration of war, the Brazilian government adopted a restrictive interpretation of the Geneva Convention of 1929, and only interned in concentration camps the prisoners of war who were found on national territory and elements closely tied to the Axis forces. In fact, according Marcondes Filho, Minister of Justice of the Estado Novo, the Convention did not refer to civilians (Perazzo, 2009, p.61).

Of a total of approximately 6 million citizens who were nationals of enemy countries Brazil removed to concentration camps, erected according to the criteria laid down in the Geneva Convention, only a handful of people, numbering no more than five thousand. In contrast, the U.S. interned in their camps about one hundred and ten thousand citizens of Japanese origin (Ibid., p.36), but the government of Getúlio Vargas resisted pressure by the United States to adopt the same procedure in Brazil.

---

2 Concerning the Battle of Stalingrad, see Marrone (2012) and Beevor (1998).

However, the Brazilian government restricted the immigrants' freedom of movement in Brazilian territory and, above all, from speaking their own language in public. Nevertheless, as Angelo Trento has well observed: "it is necessary to point out... that these laws were applied with a large dose of tolerance and that a great share of the population showed benevolence, refusing to treat as an enemy people who, until the previous day, shared with them happiness, suffering, sacrifices, work and pleasure, as well as people with whom they had established family ties" (Trento, op. cit., p. 120).

A few days after the declaration of war, three Brazilian merchant ships were sunk: the Osório, Lajes and Antonico, all in the northern region of Brazil. Toward the end of the year 1942, the Porto Alegre was sunk off the coast of South Africa and the Apaloide, in the Caribbean Sea. Besides these, several other thwarted attacks were carried out by German and Italian submarines.

Immediately following the declaration of war, the FAB organised air patrols to combat enemy submarines, and the Brazilian Navy organised a system of convoys to better protect them. At that time, the FAB was expecting to receive new aircraft from the United States under the lend-lease scheme, for the purpose of anti-submarine warfare, which included Lockheed A-28 Hudsons, North American B-25 Mitchells and Catalina seaplanes (Campbell, op. cit., p.15).

It should be noted that, for the School of Aeronautics alone and solely for instruction purposes, the United States supplied Brazil with more than three hundred training aircraft from 1942 to 1944 (Incaer, op. cit., p.4). In this period, the FAB coached the expressive figure of 558 pilot officers in Brazil, and in training camps in the United States, a further 281, totalling 839.

German colonies in Brazil.

On the 2nd March 1942, the Natal Air Base was created, in Parnamirim, taking advantage of the small civil aviation infrastructure that already existed on site. This base became responsible for a triangle that stood facing the Southern theatre of operations, comprising southern Europe, northern Africa, the Caribbean and the Brazilian coast. The Parnamirim base became one of the busiest in the world and, for a period, the main and busiest North-American base outside the continental borders of the United States.

Aerial patrols to protect the maritime convoys represented a major effort for the FAB, and thousands of flight hours were performed monthly, by night and day, often in bad weather and in remote areas along hundreds of miles of coastline in search of submarines, which were very rarely sighted (Ibid., p.10).

In turn, the convoys operated by the Brazilian Navy were protected by two Brazilian naval forces: the Northeast Naval Force, which counted on the cruisers Bahia and Rio Grande do Sul, four Carioca class escort vessels, and a number of patrol and attack vessels, provided by the United States, and the South Patrol Group. The commander-in-chief of the Brazilian Navy was Admiral Dodsworth Martins, while the Northeast Naval Force was led by Admiral Alfredo Soares Dutra. The Southern Patrol Group, in turn, was headed by Commander Ernesto Araujo.

The convoys travelling along the Brazilian coast to the north were escorted to Recife by the Brazilian Navy. From Recife, they were escorted by North-American units based in Brazil, up to the island of Trinidad, in the Caribbean, where they joined the convoy system of the northern hemisphere, under the responsibility of the Americans. Heading south, the procedure was reversed; air cover was provided from Belém, Pará, to Bahia, by FAB units and by American units based in Brazil.

On the 2nd of March, 1943, the Brazilian cargo ship Afonso Pena, belonging to Lloyd Brasileiro, which had strayed from the convoy the day before, became easy prey and was sunk by the Fascist Italian submarine, the Barbarigo,[3] commanded by Lieutenant-Commander Robert Rigo, along the coast of Bahia, in Porto Seguro, killing 125 people, including crew and passengers.

From 1942 to 1945, the few ships owned by the Brazilian Navy

> participated in the inter-allied escort of 251 convoys and effected 195 exclusively Brazilian escorts. They led 2,881 Allied ships to safe harbour, totalling 14 million tonnes, over 3,895 miles of ocean, between the Rio Grande and Trinidad, in the Caribbean [...].[4]

The majority of Brazilian merchant ships sunk by German and Italian submarines were scouts, i.e. they travelled out of convoy. These were organised to compose a large number of vessels, grouped in columns spaced approximately a thousand yards apart, with the ships in the column at a distance of five hundred yards from each other (Almeida, 2010, p.305). Thus, a rectangle was maintained with the perimeter protected by the escort.

---

3 The same one that had torpedoed the Commander Lyra.
4 According to Admiral Arnold Toscano's log of the 21st of July, 1966.

In the political field, on the 28th January 1943, President Franklin Delano Roosevelt came to Natal for a meeting with President Getúlio Vargas, in order to address strategic issues and those related to military cooperation, since the objective of this meeting was the development of a joint campaign. On the occasion, Brazil adhered to the Atlantic Charter (Almeida, 1998, p.122-ss), and also settled the participation of Brazilian troops in the European theatre of war on the initiative of Getúlio Vargas.

According to Boris Fausto (op. cit., p.105)

> the decision to send the contingents – the only one among Latin American countries – resulted from a combination of factors, including the Vargas government's interest in strengthening its prestige, considering the enthusiasm of public opinion for the initiative and the desire to have an important position in the post-war negotiations, particularly within the sphere of the United Nations (UN), the organisation of which the major powers were already considering.

Vargas also saw the participation of Brazilian troops in the world conflict as projecting a historical perspective, forming part of his project of nation building, since he intended, and indeed later achieved, that troops from all over Brazil would compose the expeditionary force that was to be formed, so that the entire nation could be proud of its achievements (Bourne, op. cit., p.161).

Likewise, Vargas and Roosevelt discussed civil, economic, financial and commercial cooperation between the two countries during the military conflict. This cooperation was not, as one might imagine at first glance, unilateral on the part of the

82   DURVAL DE NORONHA GOYOS JR.

United States, since Brazil also made its contributions, such as conceding many of our limited number of cargo ships to transport goods to the United States.

Over the course of 1943, three new, modern destroyers, constructed in domestic shipyards located in Rio de Janeiro, the Greenhalgh, Marcílio Dias and Maris e Barros, were incorporated into the Brazilian fleet. Immediately, eight destroyers were transferred by the North-Americans to the Brazilian Navy.[5] With the increase the firepower of our Navy, greater responsibility was transferred to it in the South Atlantic theatre of operations.

According to Almeida (op. cit., p.317), the American fleet "convoyed 16 thousand vessels in the Atlantic, which corresponds to 16 merchant ships for every warship. The Brazilian Navy convoyed 3000 vessels, which corresponds to 50 merchant ships for every Brazilian warship." The Brazilian warship that had the greatest participation in these convoys was the corvette Caravellas, with 77 missions.

Similarly, the FAB had organised their patrols to combat submarines into three groups of squadrons: the first group based in Belém do Pará, the second group at the Galeão Air Base in Rio de Janeiro, and the third group in Florianópolis, Santa Catarina. These squadrons constantly received new equipment from the United States under the Lend-Lease, including the Lockheed PV-I Ventura (Campbell, op. cit., p.23).

Brazil lost 34 ships during World War II, of which 33 went down following the severance of diplomatic relations with the Axis on the 28th January 1942, and the onset of the state of bel-

---

5 Christened with the names of Bauru, Beberibe Bertioga, Bracuí, Babitonga, Baependi, Benavente and Bocaina.

ligerency unilaterally implemented by these countries. Among ships that were sunk, three were warships[6] and the remainder were merchant ships or of mixed function belonging to the companies Lloyd Brasileiro, Lloyd Nacional and Costeira.

During World War II, the Brazilian Merchant Navy suffered losses of more than one third of its gross tonnage, totalling 150,209 tonnes, of which 73% belonged to Lloyd Brasileiro. Brazil was the 15th country in tonnage sunk in the conflict, while Allied countries lost the expressive figure of 49 ships along the Brazilian coast during the same period.

Moreover, in accordance with a detailed survey undertaken by Admiral Arthur Oscar Saldanha da Gama, conducted on the archives of the German Submarine Command, it was determined that

> in all, 66 attacks by the Brazilian Navy on German submarines were recorded in the South Atlantic, which resulted in damage to or the sinking of 18 submarines along the Brazilian coast, of which nine – U-128, U-161, U-164, U-199, U-513, U-590, U-591, U-598 and U-662 – were officially registered by the German navy as having been sunk by the Brazilian Navy.[7]

---

6 The auxiliary ship Vital de Oliveira, the corvette Camaquã, and the cruiser Bahia.
7 *Revista Marítima Brasileira*, year LXXI, Oct./Dec. of 1951. Rio de Janeiro: Naval Press, Ministry of the Navy, 1952.

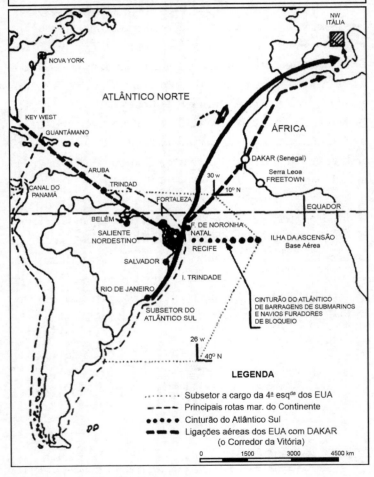

Naval warfare on the Brazilian coast.

5
THE FEB CAMPAIGN IN ITALY

On the 31st August 1942, when Brazil declared war on Germany and Italy, the Brazilian Army consisted of around 18,000 men in the northeast of the country, a contingent so limited that was not even enough to protect the air bases. However, the Brazilian army had no intention of passing the war restricted to limited domestic defence (Campbell, op. cit., p.25), a position that reflected the guidance of Getúlio Vargas, who took the initiative to insist, with Roosevelt, that Brazil send a military contingent to fight alongside the Allies in the European theatre of operations. Roosevelt agreed for several reasons, but mainly because the presence of Brazilian troops fighting under American command would strengthen the leadership of the United States in the region.

President Vargas took that decision based on his keen political instincts, but also inspired by an analysis by his foreign minister, Oswaldo Aranha, according to whom Brazil's partici-

86 DURVAL DE NORONHA GOYOS JR.

pation in the conflict would allow the country to improve its position in the global political arena,[1] in addition to consolidating its superiority in South America, providing better cooperation with the United States, reinforcing its influence on Portugal and its colonial possessions, developing its sea and air power, developing basic industry, and expanding infrastructure and exploiting domestic oil.

With the agreement signed between Getúlio Vargas and Franklin Delano Roosevelt in January 1943, regarding sending Brazilian troops to the European theatre of war, General Ord Gareshe was sent to Brazil, as a representative of the United States, in order to negotiate the details of Brazil's participation. He concluded that Brazil was determined to fight and that Brazilian troops would perform well following four to eight months training (Campbell, ibid.). Furthermore, Getúlio Vargas also agreed to place the Brazilian troops under the strategic command of the U.S. Army. The government of Brazil also signed an agreement with the United States with respect to a tentative figure of sixty thousand Brazilian combatants for the European theatre of war, i.e. an armed force composed of three divisions, a rather ambitious number considering that, in 1943, the country had a total of only ninety thousand armed men.

On the 9th August 1943, the Brazilian Expeditionary Force was created, denominated the *1ª Divisão de Infantaria Expedicionária* (DIE, 1st Expeditionary Infantry Division), which was structured by three infantry regiments: the Sampaio Regiment of the Vila Militar of Rio de Janeiro, the 6th Regiment of Cacapava, São Paulo, and the 11th Regiment of São João del Rei, Minas

---

1 Frank D. McCann. *Brazil and World War II: The Forgotten Ally.* The University of New Hampshire. Available at: www.tau.ac.il/eial/VI

THE CAMPAIGN OF THE BRAZILIAN EXPEDITIONARY FORCE... 87

Gerais. The artillery came from regiments based in the states of Rio de Janeiro and São Paulo, while the engineer corps consisted of the 6th Engineer Battalion from Aquidauana, Mato Grosso (De Moraes, 2005, p.26-ss). The FEB lacked battle tanks, a severe equipment deficiency for the contemplated operations.

The Cavalry of the FEB was formed by the 1st Reconnaissance Squadron, organized from the 2nd Motor Mecanized Regiment, based in Rio de Janeiro. This Squadron was equipped with the M-9 Greyhound armoured vehicle, of which it had 15 units. It was commanded by two FEB officials. The first one was Capitan Flávio Franco Ferreira, replaced, in Italy, by Capitan Plinio Pitaluga, a Brazilian with Italian origin. The 1st Reconnaissance Squadron had 218 enlisted personnel and officials.

On the other hand, the 1st Health Battalion was organized with the sanitary divisions from São Paulo and Rio de Janeiro. The special troops, in turn, were composed of companies from headquarters, maintenance, logistics, transmissions, police, as well as the music band division (idem, op. cit., p.27).

On the 9th July 1943, Allied troops landed in Sicily, on the beaches close to the city of Gela, on the south of the island, rapidly repelling a counterattack by the German and Italian troops. Palermo, the capital of the region, was taken on the 24th July of that year, after a bombardment destroyed the port and the city centre.[2]

On the 3rd September 1943, Allied forces, commanded by U.S. General George S. Patton and British General Bernard Montgomery, invaded the Italian peninsula via the Strait of Messina from Sicily, as Garibaldi had done, disembarking in the

---

2 Reconstruction of the area took six decades to complete.

88 DURVAL DE NORONHA GOYOS JR.

south of the country, in the Calabria region, with one hundred and fifty thousand men, four thousand aircraft and six hundred tanks.

Winston Churchill had convinced the Americans to invade the European continent through Italy, with the goal of achieving greater mutual attrition between Germany and the Soviet Union.

Churchill, whose soaring rhetoric often concealed nefarious intentions, denominated Sicily – an island off the coast of Africa, where the operation initiated – as the "soft belly" of Italy.[3]

The allied troops had come from a successful campaign in the theatre of operations in North Africa, comparatively far less important in relation to the European theatre, and which only had (negative) strategic repercussions for Italy because of its imperialist policy and casualties of one hundred thousand soldiers and losses of 300 thousand combatants captured. Fascist Italy, in addition to its military credibility, also lost 26 divisions in the North African Campaign, half of its air force and its inventory of tanks (Hastings, op. cit., p.109).

On the 7th October 1943, Lt. Gen. João Batista Mascarenhas de Moraes, seen as "a quiet man, whose lack of political ambition pleased Getúlio" (Bourne, op. cit., p.161), was appointed commander of the FEB. As a result of the understandings held with representatives of the United States, this country was responsible for providing half of the equipment and training for an infantry division and providing all their needs in the theatre of war.

---

3 Churchill, who wrote in Mussolini's newspaper, *Il Popolo d'Italia*, in a speech delivered at the Queen's Hall, London, in 1933, called the Italian dictator "the greatest existing legislator" and used the following terms: *"The Roman genius is impersonated in Mussolini, the greatest law-giver among living men..."*

The difficulties in training were numerous.[4] Firstly, the Brazilian military doctrine, made obsolete by the tactical developments of World War II, had been inspired by French missions for decades. In addition, the arms of the Brazilian army were part French, part German, with items from several other countries, including Denmark. It was necessary to recruit staff, and adaptation to the American system and the modern war movement represented a considerable challenge, principally regarding the lack of appropriate equipment.

Another issue was that the various indispensable manuals had to be translated and, besides this difficulty, gathering all the troops in Rio de Janeiro for joint training was also no easy task, and this was only possible in March 1944; however, there was an aggravating factor, because this training did not take into account the mountainous terrain of the future theatre of operations, nor the typical climatic conditions of the Italian winter. In other words, "the training of the Expeditionary Force was precarious, since the concentration of troops was very late, beginning in January 1944 and lasting until March, leaving only April and May for training the troop as a division (Albino, 2010, p.321), and there was no training camp that could hold an entire division.

By July 1943, a first contingent of Brazilian officers, consisting of 30 soldiers, went to the United States for the purpose of receiving training; others followed thereafter. Later that year, General Mascarenhas de Moraes (op. cit., p.32) visited the battlefields in Africa and Italy, leaving a group of observers in the headquarters of the Fifth U.S. Army.

---

4 Other peripheral countries that participated in the conflict, such as Australia, also had training difficulties, as demonstrated by the campaign in Singapore. The then colonies, such as India and South Africa, also had greater difficulty with the discipline of their troops.

90 DURVAL DE NORONHA GOYOS JR.

Under the orders of General Mascarenhas de Moraes, there were General Euclides Zenóbio da Costa, commander of the Infantry, General Cordeiro de Farias, commander of the Artillery, and General Olympio Falconière da Cunha, responsible for the non-divisional elements. The intelligence chief was Lieutenant Colonel Amaury Kruel, and Lieutenant Colonel Humberto Castello Branco was responsible for war operations.

There was a high number of volunteers to join the FEB and these were submitted to rigorous selection tests for the time. Many candidates were rejected. The mass antifascist struggle ensured the expansion of democratic space and made possible the reorganisation of the popular democratic movement and the Communist Party of Brazil, which advised its members to come forward as volunteers (Buonicore & Ruy, op. cit., p.75). Among the women volunteers who served in nursing corps of the FEB was Clarice Lispector, who would later become one of Brazil's greatest writers.

Due to high number of components, the FEB could not be sent to the Italian theatre at the same time. The first contingent, consisting of 5,075 soldiers embarked in Rio de Janeiro on the 30th June 1944; this group, of which General Mascarenhas de Moraes was a part, was composed of the 6th Infantry Regiment and some precursor and support units. The trip took about three weeks to the port of Naples in Campania, having driven overland to the region of Pisa, reaching the major deep-water port located at Livorno, in Tuscany, central Italy.

The number of FEB effectives was 25,334 persons, representatives of 21 Brazilian states (De Moraes, op. cit., p.313), including 20 women, who served as nurses in the health units; however, the number of actual combatants was 15,265. They were transported in U.S. ships and escorted by the Brazilian Navy, the FAB and units of the U.S. Navy. FEB members in-

THE CAMPAIGN OF THE BRAZILIAN EXPEDITIONARY FORCE... 91

cluded numerous Italian, German, Japanese, Polish and Lebanese descendants, among others. As Sergeant Ruy de Noronha Goyos well remembers, in the FEB, what most prevailed were "mestizos" originating from all over Brazil.[5]

Among the young Brazilian *"febiano"*[6] officers of foreign origin was Second Lieutenant Rubens Resstel, 2nd Howitzer Group of the Artillery Division, whose grandfather was a German from Hannover and grandmother was an Italian from Verona, who had just graduated from the Realengo Military Academy. Second Lieutenant Resstel served with extraordinary bravery and was wounded three times in action.[7] In the Italian campaign, he was awarded the Silver Star, one of the highest honours of the U.S. Army, the Combat Cross 1st Class, the *Medalha de Sangue do Brasil* and the Campaign Medal.[8]

In addition, the FEB troops were racially integrated, not segregated into battalions of whites, blacks and Japanese, like the forces of the United States. The black American soldiers were excluded from the honour guards and always presented themselves separately, often with inferior equipment, until the end of the war. Worse than this, for a long time, the U.S. Army even segregated blood for transfusion.

A photo of one aspect of the embarkation of the FEB in Rio de Janeiro, showing black and white soldiers together, caused furore in the United States and was used by sunday press media

---

5 Personal testimony given to the author, on the 1st June 2013.

6 *Febianos* is the most commonly used designation for members of the Brazilian Expeditionary Forces.

7 Testimony of the namesake son of General Resstel, given to the author on the 1st June 2013.

8 "Morre aos 88 anos o General Rubens Resstel de Problemas Cardíacos" [*General Rubens Resstel dies of Heart Disease, Aged 88*], AE 27th July 2008. Available at: www.bahdigital.com.br/site/news/reporteb

92   DURVAL DE NORONHA GOYOS JR.

to promote racial integration in that country. The *Afro-American* from Baltimore, published a photo with the headline "Blacks and whites fight together for Brazil, why not for the United States?"[9]

The *febianos* were disgusted by racial segregation among U.S. troops and welcomed wounded blacks of the U.S. Army in the Brazilian medical service. In turn, injured black Americans preferred to be treated by Brazilian medical services because they were not treated with discrimination due to their colour (Rosenheck, op. cit.). Thus, racial integration in the Brazilian troops was used to promote the campaign for civil rights of blacks in America during and after World War II.

When they arrived in Italy, the FEB troops found a country in full civil war because Mussolini had been deposed on the 8th September 1943 and the new Italian government had signed an armistice with the Allies. Italy was ruined and, as losers in the conflict, the Italians no longer identified with Mussolini; they hated him as much as they had loved him (Innocenti, op. cit., p.117).

Mussolini was freed by the Germans and installed in the so-called Republic of Salò. Fascist troops in significant numbers fought alongside the Germans, who effectively controlled the areas of Italy not yet liberated. Gradually, Italian troops were also introduced on the Allied side, which already had a significant number of *partigiani* supported by some five thousand Soviet volunteers (Semiriaga et al., 1985, p.31). A genuine civil war was also being fought.

At the time, Italy was ravaged by war and the Italians went through untold hardships, since the cities had been heavily bombarded by the artillery and aviation of the Allied forces

---

9 Uri Rosenheck, Olive Drab. "Black and White: The Brazilian Expeditionary Force, The U.S. Army and National Racial Identity." Available at: lasa.international.pitt.edu, 210.

and were semi-destroyed. The number of Italian civilians killed (64,000) in Allied bombardments was greater than that in England under the *Luftwaffe* attacks (43,000).

The Italian people, despondent, went cold, hungry, thirsty, but did not lose the sense of criticism and sang:

Mussolini, il Duce who leads us,
by day, there is no bread and
by night there is no light.

The FEB was one of 20 Allied divisions to fight in that period of the Italian theatre of operations, integrated with the 4th Corps of the U.S. Army, under the U.S. Fifth Army. Among the troops who fought beside the FEB were segregated units of the U.S. 92nd (black) and 442nd (Japanese) Divisions as well as anti-fascist Italian troops, those from the British colonies and the French.

The *febianos* underwent their baptism of fire on the 16th September 1944, when the Brazilian artillery went into action. On the occasion, the U.S. Army in the region operated in a critical situation due to the lack of infantry, since seven divisions had been transferred to the French theatre. Brazilian troops were reinforced by three tank companies of the Fifth U.S. Army.

At the onset of its activities, less FEB encountered difficulties since the German troops were withdrawing to a fortified defensive position further north, in the mountainous region of the Tuscan Apennines, called the Gothic Line.[10] Subsequently, having adopted the new fortified positions up in the mountains, the Germans began their customary tenacious, systematic resistance.

---

10 The Gothic Line runs from Pisa, on the Tuscan coast, to Rimini, on the Adriatic coast, cutting the Italian peninsula from west to east, but it was mostly located in the mountainous terrain of the Apennines.

94 DURVAL DE NORONHA GOYOS JR.

German troops received instructions from Berlin to deal with the members of the FEB with extreme harshness, in order to demoralise them and to be able to display them to other Latin American countries, since Brazilians were the only force from the region operating in the European theatre of war; such determination was encouraged by Nazi racism.

Horrified to this day by this event, Sergeant Ruy de Noronha Goyos reports,[11] with a profound sense of rancour, that the corpses of the Brazilian expeditionaries who fell in combat were mined with artefacts by German troops, so as to cause casualties in the medical service of the Brazilian Army. Appropriate measures were successful taken, but the sense of outrage at the debasement of the body of fallen heroes persisted and it still lives in our memory.

The first Italian city to be liberated by the FEB was Massarosa, on the 16th September 1944, which was, and still is, an important rail and road junction. This city is located in the foothills of the Apennines, at the end of a narrow coastal strip which connects Pisa, Tuscany, Genoa, in Liguria, and through which, since the days of Rome, passes the north-south connection in the northwest Mediterranean coast of Italy.

Moreover, Massarosa controlled the highway and railroad that led from the coast to Pistoia, Florence and Bologna, an important industrial and commercial centre close to the Adriatic sea. Some historians have only attributed tactical missions to the FEB, but only a superficial geographical knowledge is sufficient to envision the strategic importance of Massarosa.

At a later phase, the cities of Bozzano and Quiesa were liberated, where General Zenóbio Costa established his general

---

11 Personal testimony given to the author, on the 1st June 2013.

headquarters.[12] Next, the FEB began operating in the Serchio valley, in progressively more rugged terrain, which facilitated its defence. The Serchio River rises in the Apennine mountains and runs south toward Lucca, flowing into the Mediterranean, north of Pisa. To get to Lucca, the river passes through the region where FEB troops operated, called Garfagnana,[13] one of the most inhospitable areas on the Italian peninsula, since it combines high mountains, deep valleys and dense vegetation.

In this difficult operation, the FEB achieved victories at Camaiore, Monte Prano and Barga. In that region, at that time, the experienced, veteran German 148th Division operated supported by the fascist divisions *Itália, San Marco* and *Monte Rosa*, and counted on elements of several other idiosyncratic fascist groups. The 148th was the only German division that was left intact in the theatre of operations on the Italian peninsula.

It is worth noting that Italy had never been conquered in the south-north direction, since even Hannibal and Napoleon had invaded the peninsula in the opposite direction. Next, the FEB passed through the river Rhine valley, within operating range of the German artillery, because the new Brazilian goal was the ensemble Belvedere-Torracia-Monte Castelo, very high mountain positions that dominated access to the important city of Bologna, in the west/east direction.

From November 1944 to February 1945, the Brazilian troops dominated the defence of Mount Belvedere, located northeast of the Serchio valley, an equally mountainous region where German forces had positioned themselves due to the advantage conferred by the rough terrain, protecting the flank of the defence of Bologna. In the conquest of Mount Belvedere, private Menassés

---

12 The division headquarters was located near Pisa.

13 The region is currently know for the local radical sports practice.

96 DURVAL DE NORONHA GOYOS JR.

de Aguiar Barros, from a traditional family of the country side of the state of São Paulo, died bravely in combat and was awarded the *Croix de Guerre* and the *Medalha de Sangue do Brasil*.

Subsequently, the *febianos* conquered Torracia and reached the crest of Monte Castelo with FAB air support; a very hard campaign fought in the depths of the harsh winter, with temperatures below -20°C, without adequate clothing, in adverse terrain and against a troop of seasoned veterans.

According to Sergeant Ruy de Noronha Goyos,[14] who fought in the region as part of the 6th Engineer Battalion of the FEB, the uniforms of Brazilian troops were made of denim, *"brinzinho"*[15], normal tissue, while the U.S. troops who fought in the region were equipped with waterproof uniforms, suitable for use in snow; furthermore, the fact that the Americans were skilled in the use of skis and had been trained in the mountains of the state of Colorado in the United States also carried weight. Brazilian soldiers, however, had never experienced snow, and some had never even experienced cold temperatures.

From the 16th September 1944, onwards the FEB conquered the enemy

> sometimes inch by inch, over 400 kilometres [(250 miles)] from Lucca to Alessandria, between the valleys of the Serchio, Reno and Panaro rivers, and in the plain of Padua, and liberated more than 50 villages and towns. Montese was the first Italian city liberated by the FEB, on the 14th April 1945, in the course of a battle that lasted three or four days and left the region in a state of desolation and destruction...[16]

---

14 Personal testimony given to the author on the 1st June 2013.
15 A lightweight denim appropriate for warm climates and frequently used in children's clothes.
16 La Força Expedicionária Brasileira – FEB. Available at: www.museo. comune.montese.mo.it

In this operation, the 1st Motor Reconnaissance Squadron stood out, under the command of the then Capitain Plinio Pitaluga.

According to General Mark Clark (1995, p.443), commander of the U.S. Fifth Army, the main Allied force, which the FEB integrated and under which it operated, together with American, Indian, South African and British armed forces, "the FEB opened impressive holes in the German defences and conquered Monte Castelo, after eradicating the enemy from Mount Belvedere and Monte della Terracia."

According to records at the *Museo Storico Montese* (Montese Museum of History), "relationships with the civilian population were also frequent and positive, marked by a climate of friendship and warmth: on the part of Brazilians, assistance and supplies to civilians often went well beyond the limits set by the Allies".[17]

According to the testimony of Sergeant Ruy de Noronha Goyos,[18] in that very rigorous winter, German troops then in retreat took all food resources and means of sustenance from the civilian population. In accordance with his memories of that period, the state of the local population was critical, and the condition of the children was so grievous that it moved the *febianos*, initially, to share their own rations, and later, to organise a system of emergency relief.

In recognition of the fraternal relationship that was established with the soldiers of the FEB, Montese dedicated to them Room 5 of the History Museum and two monuments,[19] a street

---

17 La Força Expedicionária Brasileira – FEB, op. cit., V. nota 93.
18 Personal testimony given to the author on the 1st June 2013.
19 There are other monuments in Italy in honour of the FEB, including one titled "Liberazione" with Monte Castelo in the background.

98 DURVAL DE NORONHA GOYOS JR.

and a square.[20] Moreover, FEB established a relationship of close collaboration with the Italian forces of resistance against the Germans, the heroic *partigiani*,[21] in particular with the *Brigata Giustizia e Libertà* and the *Divisione Garibaldi*, the latter formed by Italian Communist Party cadres.

From Montese, the FEB advanced from the east, close to the Adriatic, where they were, returning westward from whence they departed, back towards the Mediterranean and the port of Genoa, to try to cut off the withdrawal of German troops who were heading to northern Italy, in the direction of Germany.

During this difficult advance over 130 miles (209 km), achieved in a few days in adverse conditions, the FEB liberated Alessandria, an important junction located just 31 miles (50 km) northwest of Genoa, a strategic objective of the Allies, and Fornovo (Clark, op. cit., p.461). Genoa fell, finally liberated by the *partigiani*, due to the collapse of the German defences on the Eastern Front of Europe.

On the 26th April 1945, the FEB again came into contact with the German 148th Division, which included the fascist division *Bersaglieri*, from the Republic of Salò, pressuring it in Fornovo, placing them under siege and cutting off their retreat to the North and cornering them to the rear, against the Apennines, until their unconditional surrender[22] signed by the German General Otto Pizo Fetter, accompanied by Italian fascist General Mario Carloni. In this operation, the 1st Motor Reconnaissance Squadron again stood out, under the command of

---

20 La Força Expedicionária Brasileira – FEB, op. cit., V. nota 93.

21 According to data compiled in the post-war period, there was a period in which Brazilian troops commanded a total of about 100,000 *partigiani* in the Italian theatre of war (Monti, op. cit., p.46).

22 Paranaense Legion of the FEB, Itinerary of the Brazilian Expeditionary Force on the Italian Campaign, Imprensa Oficial, n.d.

THE CAMPAIGN OF THE BRAZILIAN EXPEDITIONARY FORCE... **99**

Capitain Plinio Pitaluga, who "acting magnificent and boldly, as a pursuit troop", held the front line of the German division.

The FEB received a contingent of 20,573 German soldiers and Italian fascists,[23] including two generals and 892 officers, 80 guns, 5000 vehicles and 4000 horses. This number was equivalent to the FEB's own contingent; an extraordinary feat! The then *febiano* Lieutenant Salli Szainberber participated in the episode, serving with the Artillery Division, which participated in the siege together with the 6th Infantry Regiment.

In the final phase of the campaign in Italy, troops of the FEB arrived in Turin, in the Piedmont region, on the 2nd May 1945, and later advanced to the Italian border with France, again in the mountainous region of the Mediterranean Alps, where they had a joint meeting with French troops.

The FEB emblem stylised a snake smoking a pipe, a firm and humorous response to a comment attributed to Adolf Hitler when Brazil declared war on Germany and Italy, according to whom it would be easier for a snake to smoke than for Brazilian troops to make a difference on the battlefield.

FEB casualties during the campaign in the Italian theatre of war comprised 467 dead, including 13 officers and 444 enlisted men; 2,722 wounded and injured; and 35 prisoners, including one officer and 34 enlisted men. Among the surnames of Brazilian killed in combat, alongside hundreds of typically Brazilian names, such as Aguiar Barros,[24] are the surnames of immigrant families, including Marchetti, Berti, Zechin, Nardeli, Tomazini, Naliato, Randi, Pavani, Lorenzi, Nonato and Maroti, of

---

23 Among whom, the Fascist General Mario Carloni.

24 The uncle of Professor José Manuel Barros de Aguiar, a native of São José do Rio Preto, former president the 11th of August Academic Centre of the Largo de São Francisco Faculty of Law, and important Brazilian jurist.

Italian origin; Hisserich, Göering, Piffer, Schade, Stobl, Weber, Wolff and Holder, of German origin; Higaskino of Japanese origin; Jamil and Dagli, Jacob Cheib and Assad Feres, of Lebanese origin (De Moraes, op. cit., 260-ss).

On the 10th September 1944, the transfer of Brazilian aviation began, represented by the 1st FAB Fighter Group, commanded by Squadron leader Nero Moura, to Italy, terminating on the 7th October of that year, at the Tarquínea Air Base, near Rome. Later, the group was moved to Pisa, further north, to a location much closer to the operations, and the 1st FAB Fighter Group was equipped with American aircraft P-47 Thunderbolt, of excellent quality, robust fighter planes, which weighed around 7 tons each and were equipped with an engine of over two thousand horse power. The P-47 had a recognized quality (Perdigão, 1945, p. 46 –ss), and operated as fighter bombers, due to the virtual elimination of the Nazi aviation from the war theatre.

The objectives of the FAB Fighter Group included three main purposes:

a) Support for ground forces on the front;
b) Isolation of the battlefield by systematic disruption of the vias of communication in the Po valley; and
c) Destruction of enemy military and industrial installations in northern Italy.[25] The first order of the day to the 1st FAB Fighter Group, on October 14th 1944, advised that " in the history of human kind, it was given to us the privilege of being the first South American air force to cross oceans and fly over Europeans battle fields." (Perdigão, op. cit., p. 53). The Group had trained in Brazil,

---

25 "O Brasil na II Guerra Mundial" [*Brazil in World War II*]. Available at: www.brasilinter.com.

Panama and the United States. The Emblem of the 1st FAB Fighter Group, created by Colonel Geraldo Guia Aquino, displayed an ostrich resembling Lieutenant Pedro de Lima Mendes, over white clouds – aviator's floor. The blue shield containing the Southern Cross, constellation which simbolized the Brazilian Armed Forces. The expression "senta a pua!", which was a slang back in those days for "let's move ahead!", is the war cry of the 1st FAB Fighter Group, equivalent to the British "tally ho" and French "a la chasse!".

The other FAB unit, that participated in the conflict in Italy was the 1st Liaison and Observation Squadron, *"Olho Nele"* [lit. Eyes on him], commanded by Flight lieutenant João Afonso Fabrício Belloc and equipped with L4-H Piper Cub aircraft. The *"Olho Nele"* operated with the FEB Artillery Division as observers and directors of rounds.

In early November, the FAB Fighter Group began operating squadrons entirely formed of Brazilian officers and receiving their own objectives of attack; moreover, their supporting elements were also Brazilian. Among them, there was a medic corps with about a ten officers and six nurses.

The 1st FAB Fighter Group incursions were carried out with 8 aircrafts, divided into two sections of four airplanes. Each airship would carry two bombs weighing 500 pounds each and eight machine guns. On the 6th of the same month, the Air Force suffered its first fatal loss in combat: Flying Officer Cordeiro e Silva.

In December, the group moved to the Pisa Air Base, the closest to the area of fighting, as noted previously, but still up to 124 miles (200 km) from the area of operations. In separate incidents, two Brazilian aviators (Flight lieutenant Theobald Kopp and Flying Officer Danilo Moura) were shot down in

102 DURVAL DE NORONHA GOYOS JR.

combat by German anti-aircraft guns and joined the *partigiani* operating in that region. Captain Theobaldo Kpp participated along with the *partigiani* of Frabbrico (RE) in some guerrilla actions and then joined the Allied troops that headed North. In turn, Pilot officer Marcos Magalhães was shot down and taken prisoner by the Germans, but managed to escape.

Regarding the participation of the FAB in conquering Monte Castelo, General Mascarenhas de Moraes (op. Cit., p.352) noted that "FAB airplanes had devastated German resistance in Mazzancana, in a bold participation in the land combat and an unforgettable example of the union of expeditionaries of the air and land."

Among the 48 pilots of the FAB Fighter Group, a total of 22 casualties occurred. The FAB Liaison and Observation Squadron, who worked with the artillery of the FEB, flew no less than 682 war missions (Incaer, op. cit., p.20). The FAB Fighter Group executed a total of 445 missions in the theatre of war in Italy, with 2,546 flight sorties. On their missions they destroyed 1,304 motorised vehicles, 250 railroad cars, 8 armoured cars, 25 railroad, road bridges and factories, and 31 fuel and ammunition depots. Using comparative analysis, the FAB Fighter Group presented the best performance among the Allied forces in that theatre of military operations at that time, an extraordinary achievement.

For example, from the 6th to the 29th April 1945, the FAB Fighter Group flew 5% of the missions run by the 22nd Command, but was responsible for 15% of the vehicles destroyed, 28% of the bridges destroyed, 36% of damaged fuel deposits and 85% of damaged ammunition depots (Incaer, ibid.). At that time, Nazi aviation had little presence in the skies over Italy, but the German flak batteries were very effective.

In all their missions, the Brazilian fighter planes faced strong resistance from enemy air defence, a situation exacerbated because the attacks were made at very low altitude. The planes of the Fighter Group were hit once every 17 sorties and the number of daily sorties was approximately 20.

Statistics proved that the percentage of loss in missions carried out by FAB, that is, flying low using the plane's submachine guns, is considerably higher than the percentage obtained in escorting or interception missions.(Perdigão, op. cit, p. 80). The German anti-aircraft artillery was formed by enormous 88mm cannons, which could shoot almost horizontally against airplanes flying at low altitude (Perdigão, op. cit., p. 85).

In the short period that elapsed between the 11th of November 11 1944, and the 2nd May 1945, when the FAB Fighter Group flew its last combat mission in the Italian skies, Flight officer José Rebelo Meira de Vasconcelos flew no fewer than 93 missions on that front.[26] The number of missions was so high, given the fact that the Germans required only 3 days to fix all damage caused to the targets, which demanded recurrent attacks.

"Senta a Pua", slang of the time for full power, has become the battle cry of the Fighter Group. The symbol displayed an ostrich, a bird that eats everything, with a machine gun and a shield with the Southern Cross on it, upon the clouds, surrounded by a green and yellow border. Brigadier Ruy Moreira Lima (1989, p.40), in his classic work on the operative of the FAB in Italy, tells the story of its creation.

During the campaign in Italy, the FAB lost about three pilots per month in diverse casualties, including those shot down and killed, missing and captured pilots. The bravery of the compo-

---

26 Subsequently, Meira became a fighter instructor at the Santa Cruz Air Base, in the city of Rio de Janeiro.

104 DURVAL DE NORONHA GOYOS JR.

nents of the 1st Fighter Division of the FAB, coupled with their extraordinary sense of duty, provided the group the unusual honour of a U.S. Presidential Citation.

In the proposed Presidential Unit Citation, the commander of the 350th Fighter Group, Colonel Ariel Nielsen of the U.S. Air Force, thus justified:

> This group entered combat at a time when anti-aircraft opposition against fighter-bombers was at its height. Their losses have been constant and heavy and they have had few substitutions. As they became less numerous each one began to fly more often, exposing himself with greater frequency... In my opinion, their attacks on the San Benedetto region, on April 22nd, 1945, helped pave the way for the beachhead established by the Allies in the same region. In order to complete this, the 1st Brazilian Fighter Group, in their deeds, exceeded those of all other groups and suffered serious losses.[27]

Among the eight brave FAB aviators killed in combat in the Italian theatre, was Flying officer Rolando Rittmeister, a Brazilian of German origin (Moraes, op. cit., p.270). On the other hand, the Fighter Group's first casualty, which occurred in training while still in Panama, was Pilot officer Dante Isidoro Gastaldoni, a Brazilian of Italian origin. The FAB Fighter Group returned to Brazil two months after the end of the war.

In turn, Flying officer Aurelio Vieira Sampaio died south of Milan, while attacking enemy fortifications. The fire from German flak shot him down while flying his 16th war mission and he was awarded the *Cruz de Valor* of the FAB and the Air Medal (USA). Flying officer Luiz Lopes Dornelles was killed by flak

---

27 Available at: <www.tropasdeelite.xpg.com.br/FAB-1GAVC.htm>.

THE CAMPAIGN OF THE BRAZILIAN EXPEDITIONARY FORCE... 105

while carrying out an attack on his 89th war mission.[28] Two other Brazilian pilots, Frederico Santos e Armando de Souza, were shot down and killed in April.

Other Brazilian pilots were shot down in combat but survived. Flying officer Josino Maia of Assisi was one of them, shot down while flying his 41st war mission, south of Milan, in January 1945. He tried to escape, but was taken prisoner by the Germans and was transferred to Nuremberg and, later, to Musberg. He was decorated with the *Cruz de Sangue do Brasil*, the *Cruz de Aviação do Brasil*, the United States Air Medal and the United Kingdom Distinguished Flying Cross.

In turn, Flight lieutenant Ismael da Motta Paes, shot down on his 24th war mission, was captured "after local inhabitants refused to receive him in their house". He was, after interrogations, taken to a prisoner's camp in Frankfurt and then interned at STALAGLUFT 1, where he remained until the end of the war, at which point he had lost 14 kilos. Flight lieutenant Roberto Brandini, shot by German anti-aircraft and hit in the head by a grenade shard, was captured and submitted to a surgery while held prisoner. In the same way, the 2nd Flight Lieutenant Marcos Coelho de Magalhães, was shot and, after jumping with a parachute, fractured both ankles and was held prisoner (Perdigão, op. cit., p. 106).

The dictator Benito Mussolini was captured by the Italian *partigiani* on the 27th April 1945, carrying a significant amount of gold and pounds sterling, while trying to escape to Germany in a German convoy and dressed as a German soldier. He was executed the next day (Hibbert, op. cit., p.310-ss). His mutilated body was exposed in the Piazzale Loreto in Milan, along with

---

28 Flying officers John Richardson Cordeiro e Silva, Oldegard Olsen Sapucaia, Waldir Paulino Pequeno de Mello, José Maurício Campos de Medeiros and Gustavo Frederico dos Santos also died in combat.

106 DURVAL DE NORONHA GOYOS JR.

that of his mistress, Claretta Petacci, in the same place where the Germans had shot 15 members of the Italian resistance, leaving their bodies exposed for 24 hours (Monti, op. cit., p. 293).

Thus ended the unfortunate adventure of fascism, which brought so much disgrace, misfortune and suffering to the Italian people. Likewise, it drew to a close the artificial and bizarre action of the Republic of Salò,[29] a fascist government established by Germans in the northern part of the country and controlled by them following the surrender of Italy on the 28th August 1943.

In mid-April, the Red Army troops, under the command of Marshal Georgy Zhukov, reached the German capital Berlin (Roberts 2012, p.224-ss), a city whose population before the war of four and a half million had dropped by this time to about three million, two million of whom were women and one hundred and twenty thousand were children. The Soviet troops had 77 infantry divisions supported by 3,155 tanks and about fifteen thousand pieces of artillery.

At that time, the Allied troops had not yet reached the line of the Pó River in northern Italy, because of the tenacious German resistance, the difficult terrain and operations and strong forces which included no fewer than 25 of their own divisions and 5 more divisions of the Republic of Salò (Clark, op. cit.,p.451), comprising a contingent of over six hundred thousand combatants!

Thus, the final and decisive victory in the Italian theatre of operations was caused by the success of Soviet troops in Germany, when the German armed forces still resisting in northern Italy collapsed. Thus, many Italian cities, such as Genoa, Milan and Turin, were liberated by the *partigiani* even before the arrival of Allied troops.

---

29 A small town on the western shore of Lake Garda.

THE CAMPAIGN OF THE BRAZILIAN EXPEDITIONARY FORCE... **107**

Paris had been liberated by the Free French Forces and U.S. troops on the 19th August 1944. Meanwhile, also in 1944, Budapest, in Hungary, Bucharest, in Romania, Belgrade, in Yugoslavia and Sofia, in Bulgaria, were liberated by Soviet troops. Greece, Ukraine and Finland were liberated in 1944, the last two by Soviet troops (Semiriaga et al., op. cit., p.33-ss). Meanwhile, in the Pacific theatre, Manila was liberated by American troops commanded by General Douglas MacArthur on the 3rd March 1945. Singapore, however, only fell following the Japanese surrender in September 1945.

The dictator Adolf Hitler committed suicide in his bunker in Berlin, on the 1st May 1945 (Ryan, 1966, p.507). No less than six hundred and twenty five thousand Germans, including onde hundred and twenty five thousand civilians, died in the unnecessary Battle of Berlin. On the same date as Hitler's suicide, Joseph Stalin, the Soviet dictator, announced the fall of Berlin to the world (Roberts, op. cit., p.230). The German troops surrendered to Allied forces on the 8th of May, 1945, in Berlin, thus ending the European phase of World War II.[30]

Upon the cessation of hostilities, General Mark Clark sent a message to the Italian people, which resonates to this day due to the wisdom of his words and should never be forgotten:

men of many nations shed their blood in Italy in the cause of freedom. Grant that it has not been in vain. The struggle has ended, but the greater responsibility of citizenship is still in need of the support of all for the resurrection of Italy and in celebrating with honour the freedom won at such high cost.[31]

---

30 In the Asian theatre, Japan surrendered unconditionally on the 2nd of September, 1945, in Tokyo Bay.

31 *Messaggio del generale Mark Clark ai patrioti*, 5th of May, 1945.

108 DURVAL DE NORONHA GOYOS JR.

In turn, on the occasion of the surrender of German troops and fascist Allies and the consequent cessation of hostilities in the Italian peninsula, on the 3rd May 1945, General João Baptista Mascarenhas de Moraes set down in his log that would pass into History, in which he stated with great sensitivity:

> today, almost all of humanity kneels contrite, spirit revived by hope, heart resuscitated by faith and thoughts turned to rebuilding the world and the good of the whole ... And with pride without boasting, and confidence without exaggerating, let us return to our homes, to our barracks and jobs, to proceed in the holy toil to make a strong and respected Brazil, in a free and happy world (De Moraes, op. cit., p.220-ss).

On the 1st July 1944, representatives of 44 countries, including Brazil, met in Bretton Woods, New Hampshire, United States, to address global reconstruction in the post-war period and an international legal framework that would avoid a new global conflict for reasons of economic order. Thus, the World Bank was founded, to deal with the reconstruction and the International Monetary Fund with the goal of, "briefly, achieving and maintaining stability in exchange rates, facilitating the liberation of exchange restrictions and paving the way for the convertibility of currencies" (Almeida, op. cit., p.124).

The agenda of the work was defined, the debates were addressed and the conclusions were drawn by the American and British negotiators. The U.S. participants, whose principal negotiator was Harry Dexter White, were preoccupied primarily with ensuring free trade and the free flow of currencies. In turn, the British, led by John Maynard Keynes and fearing the collapse of the pound sterling, wanted to "avoid a currency war, or rather the competitive devaluation of currencies, which had occurred during the Great Depression" (Campos, 1994, p.70).

The Brazilian delegation was headed by the Minister of Finance of the Vargas government, Dr. Arthur de Souza Costa, but the chief negotiators were Eugenio Gudin and Octavio Gouveia de Bouillon, who had little success in trying to introduce the agricultural theme in the Bretton Woods negotiations, and again later in Havana, where international trade was discussed.

Ensign of the FEB.

The FEB campaign in Italy.

General Mascarenhas de Moraes, Commander of the FEB.
Source: Personal archive.

Sergeant Ruy de Noronha Goyos, of the 6th Engineer Battalion of the FEB.
Source: Personal archive.

Sergeant Ruy de Noronha Goyos and companions in Monte Castelo.
Source: Personal archive.

Ensign of the 1st Air Force Fighter Group of the FAB.

Febiano, private Menasses Barros de Aguiar in training before shipping to Italy.

Source: Personal archive.

First Lieutenant Artillery Rubens Resstel.
Source: Personal archive.

Captain Plínio Pitaluga.
Source: Personal archive.

6
EPILOGUE

The Brazilian volunteers who made up the FEB were immediately aware of the strong contradiction of fighting in the European theatre of war against dictatorships and for the prevalence of democratic values, whilst the national political regime was likened to that of Brazil's enemies. In 1944, Vargas received from his intelligence services information regarding the existence of criticism among Brazilian officers in Italy of the democratic deficit in the country (Skidmore, op. cit., p.82).

Getúlio Vargas' defects certainly did not include the lack of an acute and highly discerning political sense. Knowing the democratic aspirations of the Brazilian people and the impact of such feelings in the Armed Forces of Brazil, traditionally very close to the national values expressed by the popular classes, Vargas had given signs of the democratisation of the country.

Indeed, on the 10th November 1943, he had declared, during the celebration of the 6th anniversary of the coup of 1937, that "in an environment of peace and order, with maximum guarantees of freedom of opinion, we will readjust the political structure of the nation, we will do so in any ample and secure manner after the necessary consultations with the Brazilian people" (apud Skidmore, ibid.). Six months later, on the 15th April 1944, he would reiterate this promise.

However, Getúlio Vargas, comfortable with the Estado Novo, sought to postpone the liberalisation of the Brazilian political order indefinitely, even though, when Brazilian troops were sent to Italy, the outcome of the conflict was sealed and that it conclusion would only be a matter of time. This procrastination occurred despite the position expressed by Oswaldo Aranha, who advised him to hold general elections as soon as possible (Hilton, op. cit., p.389).

When Oswaldo Aranha left the government, Sobral Pinto unsuccessfully urged him to criticise it, since he had never done so previously, to redeem himself for past mistakes, on the basis that the regime confused the rule of Law with the laws, subjugating individual rights in favour of the single sovereign will of the governing class, suppressed completely the dignity of the human person; and improperly arrogated the power to think for everyone, to speak for everyone and to act for everyone (Dulles, op. cit., p.292).

"In January and February of 1945, with the war in Europe entering its final phase, the structure of the Estado Novo suddenly collapsed" (Bourne, op. cit., p.167). On the 18th April of that same year, Vargas decreed a general amnesty and freed all political prisoners, including Luiz Carlos Prestes and his comrades of the Communist Party, which began to operate within the law.

Eurico Dutra and Góis Monteiro, the main military chiefs, reactionary elements with a history of close affinity, admiration

THE CAMPAIGN OF THE BRAZILIAN EXPEDITIONARY FORCE...   119

and cooperation with European fascism, presented themselves as Democrats and demanded the holding of free presidential elections, scheduled for the 2nd December 1945. The election for state governments and legislatures were held together on the 6th May of the same year.

Even so, on the 29th October 1945, a military coup overthrew the government of the Estado Novo, with Vargas retiring to his farm in São Borja, Rio Grande do Sul. According to Basbaum (op. cit., p.132-ss), Góis and Dutra sought to prevent a shift to the left by Vargas, who had also re-established relations with the USSR.

The new president, José Linhares, Minister of the Federal Supreme Court (STF), who assumed the office following the coup, though evidently without a public mandate, maintained the elections on the due dates, in which General Eurico Gaspar Dutra was elected president and convened a National Constituent Assembly. The new Brazilian Constitution was promulgated on the 18th September 1946.

Dutra and Góis Monteiro, the latter Minister of the Army of the former, were against the permanence of Brazilian troops in Europe as an occupying force, and fearful of the effect of exposure of the national contingent to patriotic democratic ideas that would surely emerge in the post-war period, despite the encouragement received from the United States.

It was a provincial, second-rate decision, equal to the character of such leaders, which also greatly damaged Brazil's position of influence in the reconstruction of the new international order. In 1947, President Eurico Gaspar Dutra broke off diplomatic relations with the Soviet Union, siding with the United States in the so-called Cold War.

120 DURVAL DE NORONHA GOYOS JR.

During July and August, 1945, the troops of FEB's heroes returned to Brazil on Brazilian transports, including the Pedro I, Pedro II and the Duque de Caxias (Moraes, op. cit., p.256-7). On the occasion, in the face of demonstrations of joy at the return of the *febianos* from the Italian theatre of operations, General Clark (op. cit., p.457) commented that "the Brazilian people had a right to be proud of the performance and sacrifice of its beautiful expeditionary force, which General Mascarenhas de Moraes had led with such skill and intelligence."

In that defining moment, as observed by Boris Fausto

> Dutra and Góis quickly dealt with demobilising the expedition armies, and they were prohibited from speaking publicly and even from walking in uniform in the streets, bearing medals and decorations. In civilian life, associations of ex-combatants fought to secure their rights, but many faced employment difficulties and suffered the traumatic effects of war, including mental disorders and alcoholism.

As an immediate result of the war, a new international legal order emerged. In April 1945, at the end of the confrontation, representatives of 50 states, including Brazil, gathered at the United Nations Conference on the International Organisation in the City of San Francisco, California, to discuss the United Nations Charter, which was signed on the 26th June 1945. The UN formally came into existence on the 24th October 1945, with its headquarters in New York City (Goyos Junior, 2005 p.31).

The UN Charter is the highest ranking international treaty and provides a mechanism for the development of international law. The purposes of the UN are to maintain international peace and security, to develop friendly relations among States based on the equality and self-determination of peoples, international cooperation and the coordination of joint actions (Ibid., p.33).

The effective power of the UN is concentrated in the Security Council, composed of 15 members of the UN, of which 5 are permanent: China, Russia, France, the United Kingdom and the United States of America (Ibid., p.37). During the Yalta negotiations, from the 4th to the 18th February 1945, Roosevelt proposed that Brazil became a permanent member of the Security Council (Plokhy, 2010, p.120), an initiative that was vetoed by Joseph Stalin, because he considered the country to be a U.S. client state.

Several other specialised UN agencies were created, including the World Bank, the International Monetary Fund (IMF), UNICEF and the General Agreement on Tariffs and Trade (GATT), now known as the World Trade Organization (WTO). Gradually, an international legal order was founded that, whilst not yet perfect, is a considerable improvement on the previous anomie. More importantly, a basic system for the development of international law for the short, medium and long term, was agreed upon.

The international legal regime created from 1945 onwards contributed decisively in preventing the so-called Cold War, resulting from dividing the world into two blocks with very different visions, one led by the United States and the other by the Soviet Union, to evolve into World War III. Likewise, the UN contributed to the process of decolonisation that followed and international humanistic consciousness is very grateful to it for such decisive action.

This important decolonisation process was carried forward despite opposition from Winston Churchill, a confessed and tenacious imperialist, who publicly declared that he had not been chosen prime minister to preside over the dismantling of the British Empire. The British Empire had come to control 25% of humanity. As a result of this process, countries like India, which became independent in 1947, freed themselves from the poverty, despondency and oppression of colonial rule.

Brazil's participation in World War II, besides the military contribution itself and the supply and shipping of so-called strategic goods, aligned the democratic feelings and humanistic values of the Brazilian people with those of the allies who fought for a world founded on a supranational legal order and respect for human rights.

It is natural that Brazilian popular consciousness would desire the same for the internal legal order of the country. However, Brazil would still traverse several decades in political turmoil, facing serious challenges, before our institutions would be perfected and could head towards a solid democracy.

On the other hand, it is undeniable that the Brazilian State, its territorial unity and the national federalist regime emerged strengthened from the global conflict because of the dialectical experiences that have occurred since the Revolution of 1930. From the standpoint of the implementation of basic industry in Brazil, the decisive government policy of Vargas, with the cooperation received from the United States as part of negotiations with the country, the balance was highly positive.

With the prohibition of foreign languages in Brazil, the use of the Portuguese language was reinforced among the vast contingents of immigrants that existed in the country, who, despite the pressures brought to bear by the United States on this issue and resisted by Getúlio Vargas, were never confined to concentration camps as national enemies. The descendants of immigrants were more readily assimilated and integrated into the

THE CAMPAIGN OF THE BRAZILIAN EXPEDITIONARY FORCE... **123**

main flow of Brazilian culture, interbreeding and enriching it in all respects, including with regard to tolerance, a fundamental human virtue.

Insightful, the great Austrian writer Stefan Zweig (2008, p.117), exiled in Brazil due to Nazi racial persecution, had previously observed, in 1942, that

> like before, the Napoleonic wars indirectly created political independence, so Hitler's war created Brazilian industry and, thus, as it managed to retain its political independence, this country will know how to preserve its economic independence over the centuries.

Similarly, with the linguistic integration driven by new media from the 1950s onwards, the benign process of miscegenation intensified, promoting tolerance that marks the national culture. The closing of foreign schools obligated the Brazilian State to fill the vacuum, which was achieved with increasing success over the years. After the end of the military conflict, in general, foreign immigration to Brazil returned, including Italian, which continues to this day, "though not on the enormous scale of immigration recorded at the end of the nineteenth century."[1]

In the following years, with the redemocratisation of Brazil from 1986, the main contradiction of the country is no longer the effort to establish a democratic regime to substantiate the promotion of economic growth and social development, marked by resistance to the economic imperialism of the United States

---

1 Ambasciata d'Italia, "Presenza Italiana in Brasile - Cenni sulle collettività" [*The Italian presence in Brazil – Notes on the community*] op. cit., p.28.

124 DURVAL DE NORONHA GOYOS JR.

in the domestic sphere and opposition to the arbitrary exercise of their own reasons in international relations by that country. And as the great intellectual Austrian Stefan Zweig aptly noted (op. cit., p.123), "to all of Brazil's untapped and uncharted energies, a new one was added in recent years: consciousness of the nation's own value".

In turn, Italy emerged from the fascist experience and the war with about five hundred thousand soldiers and two hundred and fifty thousand civilians killed, with a shattered economy, with a smaller territory without Friuli-Venezia Giulia, with the population in misery, without the fascist empire (Petacco, 1995, p.296-7), but with the hope that an era of freedom, justice and social well-being could begin.

The entire Italian people committed themselves to the economic reconstruction of the country, which took no less than ten years and was known as a miracle due to the nature of the challenge. These transformations were not without social conflicts and crises in the democratic regime that was established in the country from 1946 (Magni, 1989, p.250) and in which entities that participated in the resistance to fascism had an admittedly important role.

The political reconstruction of the country continues to this day with great difficulty, as does the fight against organised crime. This unfortunately suffered a setback in the post-war period as a result of the alliance formed by the Unites States with the Mafia, to obtain the necessary logistical support and intelligence[2] for the Allied invasion of 1943. As a result, mem-

---

2 In the so-called Operation Underworld, conducted by American naval intelligence, who recruited mobsters like Lucky Luciano and Joseph Lanza.

THE CAMPAIGN OF THE BRAZILIAN EXPEDITIONARY FORCE... 125

bers of the *Onorata Società* were set up by the Americans, first as mayors in Sicily, so that they could then be lifted to positions of national responsibility in Rome.

Germany not only came out of World War II shattered, with its territory 25% smaller, but also "divided into two rival and antagonistic states" (Bandeira, 2011, p.88). Its huge population was famished and cold, deprived of basic public services and living in the open in the somber ruins of its cities. More than 7 million civilians were homeless. On the 23rd May 1949, the Federal Republic of Germany (FRG) was established, unifying the three zones occupied by the Western powers.

In the eastern zone, controlled by the Soviet Union, the German Democratic Republic (GDR) was formed, founded on the 7th October 1949 (Ibid., p.85-ss). The two states were reunified only on the 3rd October 1990, when, through the so-called Unification Treaty, "the sovereign FRG incorporated not only the GDR, which had dissolved, but also the five old *Länder* [...] on whose territories it was constituted" (Bandeira, 2009, p.204).

In 1950, Brazil and Germany signed the first post-war commercial treaty. From this date on, German companies resumed the traditional investments in Brazil. By the end of 1957, over German 130 businesses had started their activities in Brazil, among them Volkswagen of Brazil, Mercedes Benz of Brazil, MWM, Degussa and Ferrostaal. The city of São Paulo became the major recipient of German investments in the world. The German immigration flux continued, although on a smaller scale.

Similar to Germany and Italy, Japan came out of World War II not only equally ruined, but also destroyed and contaminated by the unnecessary explosion of two atomic bombs in two of its major urban centres, Hiroshima and Nagasaki, by the United

States. About six hundred thousand Japanese civilians died as a result of conventional and nuclear air strikes, and approximately five million civilians were left homeless.

Japan rebuilt it economy with its customary discipline and huge national effort, which quickly became one of the largest in the world. A Constitution was approved and a parliamentary democracy was then established, preserving the traditional monarchy. Subsequently, many Brazilians of Japanese origin were welcomed as workers in the country of origin of their ancestors without any need to leave their home in Brazil, and this intensified the human, cultural, economic and linguistic exchange between the two countries. Several Japanese democratic post-war governments have supported Brazil and, particularly the state of Sao Paulo and its capital, with funding for improvements in domestic infrastructure. Many Japanese companies have established themselves in Brazil, especially in the State of São Paulo.

In the post-war period, economic, social, political and cultural relations between Brazil, Germany, Italy and Japan evolved admirably, with intense cooperation on many levels. Today, together, our countries defend the same humanistic values and promote them both internally, within their respective territories, and internationally, in numerous global fora.

In large part, this is a result of the efforts of the men and women who composed the Brazilian Expeditionary Force, together with the extraordinary commitment and enormous sacrifice of the Brazilian people, notably because it was made spontaneously by a free, developing, independent and sovereign nation, which believed and still believes in the ideals of the time.

Thus, the account of the circumstances of the FEB campaign for the liberation of Italy and the defeat of the Axis forces constitutes a chapter of history that should not and cannot be forgotten because of all that it represents for the national consciousness, for the community of nations and their respective peoples, for good bilateral relations between Brazil and Italy, and also for the definition and preservation of the best humanistic values.

Ensign of the UN.

AFTERWORD

Dr. Walter Sorrentino[1]

Freedom is irrepressible

There are reflections that are established at the intersection of things that are necessary and things that are precious. This small literary work by Dr. Durval Noronha Goyos Jr., is one such thing. Concise and cultured, it brings to light salient episodes of nationality and the role of Brazil in the world, as well as redeeming deserved honours to the handful of Brazilian Expeditionary Force fighters and services rendered to the national and international democratic cause in those terrible years of World War II, the greatest of the twentieth century.

Nations do not live in a permanent state of passion or revolution. On the contrary, aside from normal and contradictory

---

1 Walter Sorrentino is a physician and one of the national leaders of the Communist Party of Brazil (PCdoB).

130 DURVAL DE NORONHA GOYOS JR.

development, they most often do not encounter opportunities to make great civilisational leaps; sometimes they regress demoralised, as perceived by the end of the Soviet Union in the 1990s and certain European countries nowadays.

This must be said, because Brazil lived through exciting times in the episodes portrayed, when prospects for a more autonomous nation, with social rights and freedom opened up. In a deeply contradictory manner, the Vargas Era, which began in 1930 with the Liberal Revolution, opened a historic path that led the country to modernity over the almost 50 years that it subsisted, alternating between democracy and dictatorship, by way of the communist threat. Those who were demoralised (and who demoralised the nation) were those whose proclaimed intent was to bury the Vargas Era and who produced, in the 1990s under the presidency of Fernando Henrique Cardoso, a national regression.

The years 1939 to 1945 were incubated in the capitalist crisis of 1929, the second major crisis and the largest, rivalled only by that in course in the world today. Repartition of the world into spheres of imperialist influence was undertaken, and fascism and Nazism, so clearly portrayed in this book, were the predominant regimes. It was a time of political, ideological and military confrontations that are perhaps unrepeatable (hopefully) in their radicalism.

This was set against a deep libertarian longing, both worldwide and in Brazil, under the dictatorial heel of the Estado Novo. In Europe, it assumed the form of a powerful political and social movement, the armed resistance of the *partigiani* in Italy, the internationalist republican forces in the Spanish Civil War, and the French Resistance. There was the Soviet Union's strategic reserve, whose role in the Great Patriotic War was decisive, inscribing one of the most memorable pages in military history with the victory against the siege of Stalingrad, which decided the fate of World War II. Here in Brazil, it occurred in the form of a movement of the masses that clamoured against dictatorship and for national liberation. Again, it was one of those moments of passion in which life itself was at risk, when the destinies of the collective are fused and are imposed on the individual.

One of the banners was, precisely, Brazil's intervention in support of the allied forces. In this decision, there was a strategic calculation – the victory of such forces would open up the country to democracy, which occurred in 1945. This had not escaped the strategic vision of Vargas, one of Brazil's greatest statesmen, alongside José Bonifacio and a few others, including the Baron of Rio Branco. Shrewd, they manoeuvred initially with the "Axis", then with the Allies, through the Americans. And it was not by chance that Roosevelt, during his visit to Brazil mentioned in the book, claimed that the New Deal (which pulled the United States out of the crisis) had been inspired by Getúlio Vargas. He had thus acquired successes in Brazilian industrialisation, the basis for the country's modernisation.

Hence the importance of the FEB in fighting alongside the Allies, rendering service in the liberation of Italy, since this resulted from a recurring hallmark of the defining moments of Brazilianness and the nation, which was to broadly unite people of different tendencies in an unimaginable unity, in "normal" terms. Another salient issue of this same Brazilianness was the integrationist hallmark that characterises our people. The FEB was mainly formed by descendants of Italian, German and Japanese – the very countries of the Nazi fascist axis – which largely made up Brazilian demographics, especially in São Paulo and the south of the country. There is no greater proof of democratic yearning and humanist impulse that defines us. As the book affirms, Vargas himself insisted on an FEB that expressed the contingent of the nation with enlisted men from 21 states.

This union of the people is a powerful force, achieved even among workers and sectors of the armed forces, that would come to rebel against the proto-fascist spirit of the general who succeeded Vargas, disuniting in the name of the Cold War, as if the people were some kind of internal enemy, even more dangerous than the external threats experienced by a young nation that longed to develop and take its place in the world. It is known that when this kind of ideology prevails, the nation pays the price.

There is no nation without a people, there are no people acting in defence of the nation without democracy.

This lesson was widely explored in the days described in the work of Dr. Durval Noronha, and is still valid today, in which Brazil is faced with new opportunities for national, democratic and popular affirmation, and Italy is struggling against tremendous crisis, led by political demoralisation precisely due to antinational and anti-people policies.

I hope this book promotes mutual recognition between Italians and Brazilians – which has not been lacking –, particularly in the role of the FEB in the liberation of Italy from the fascist yoke. I concede these, because this mobilisation had the prominent assistance of the communists; I concede these to Italians and Brazilians of two homelands, to those who fought there and those who supported them here, following the shining example of Giuseppe Garibaldi and Anita Garibaldi.

I pay tribute to all who have embraced the cause of liberty and the strategic interest of the nation, as Dr. Durval does today.

Because, historically, the period characterised herein has yet to be achieved here: the era of freedom and humanism, the era of justice and social progress, the era of self-determination of peoples and nations, against imperialism of any shape or kind. Such yearnings are invincible, and are illuminated by people like the friend who authored this book.

REFERENCES

AGAMBEN, Giorgio. *Carl Schmitt – Un giurista davanti a se stesso.* Vicenza: Neri Pozza, 2005.

ALBINO, Daniel. Cobras fumando: a Força Expedicionária Brasileira na Campanha da Itália. In: *O Brasil e a Segunda Guerra Mundial.* Rio de Janeiro: Multifoco, 2010.

ALMEIDA, Paulo Roberto. *Relações Internacionais e Política Externa do Brasil.* Porto Alegre: Editora da Universidade Federal do Rio Grande do Sul. 1998.

AMADO, Jorge. *O cavaleiro da esperança.* Rio de Janeiro: Record, 1987.

AMBASCIATA D'ITALIA. *Presenza Italiana in Brasile – Cenni sulle collettività.* Istituti Italiano Di Cultura: Italia, 1999.

BANDEIRA, L. A. Moniz, *O milagre alemão e o desenvolvimento do Brasil 1949-2011.* São Paulo: Editora UNESP, 2011.

BANDEIRA, Moniz. *A reunificação da Alemanha.* São Paulo: UNESP, 2009.

BARROS, Alberto da Rocha. *Que é o Facismo?* Rio de Janeiro: Gráfica Editora Laemmert AS, 1969.

136 DURVAL DE NORONHA GOYOS JR.

BASBAUM, Leôncio. *História sincera da República.* v. III. São Paulo: Alfa-Omega, 1976.

BEEVOR, Antony. *Stalingrad.* London: Viking, 1998.

BOCCA, Giorgio. *Storia d'Italia nella Guerra Fascista.* Milan: Arnaldo Mondatori, 1996.

BOSWORTH, R. J. B. *Mussolini's Italy – Life under the Dictatorship.* London: Penguin Books, 2005.

BOURNE, V. Richard. *Getúlio Vargas – A esfinge dos Pampas.* São Paulo: Geração Editorial, 2012. [*Getulio Vargas of Brazil, 1883-1954: Sphinx of the Pampas.* London: Charles Knight Ltd, 1974.]

BURNS, E. Bradford. *A History of Brazil.* 3rd ed. New York: Columbia University Press, 1993.

CAFFERY, Jefferson to Cordell Hull. Rio, 22nd April, 1939. 832.00/1255, RG59. National Archives, Washington, USA.

CAMPBELL, Keith. *Brazil in the Second World War.* Pretoria, South Africa: Unisa Centre for Latin American Studies, 1992.

CAMPOS, Roberto. *A Lanterna na Popa.* Rio de Janeiro: Top Books, 1994.

CARNEIRO, Maria Luiza Tucci. *Cidadão do mundo*: o Brasil diante do Holocausto e dos judeus refugiados do Nazifascismo (1933-1948). São Paulo: Perspectiva, 2010.

CERVO, Amado Luiz. *As relações históricas entre o Brasil e a Itália.* Brasília: UNB, 1991.

CLARK, Mark Wayne. *Mark Clark il comandante della Varmata.* Associazione Culturare Sarasota. p.443, 451, 461 & 457.

CLARK, V. Alan. *Barbarossa – The Russian-German Conflict 1941-45.* London: Weidenfeld & Nicolson, 1995.

DE GOBINEAU, Arthur. *Essai sur L'inegalité des races humaines.* Paris: Pierre Belfond, 1967. [*The Inequality of the Human Races.* New York: Howard Fertig, 1999.]

DE MORAES, J. B. Mascarenhas. "*A FEB pelo seu comandante*". Rio de Janeiro: Biblioteca do Exército, 2005. p.26, 27, 32, 220, 256, 257 & 260.

DEUTSCHER, Issaac. *Trotski – O profeta banido.* Rio de Janeiro: Civilização Brasileira, 1968. [*The Prophet Outcast, Trotsky, 1929-1940.* London: The Oxford University Press, 1949.]

THE CAMPAIGN OF THE BRAZILIAN EXPEDITIONARY FORCE... 137

DULLES, John W. F. *Sobral Pinto – "A consciência do Brasil"*. Rio de Janeiro: Nova Fronteira, 2001. [*Sobral Pinto – "The Conscience of Brazil": Leading the Attack Against Vargas (1930-1945)*. Austin: University of Texas Press, 2002].

FABBER, David. *Munich – The 1938 Appeasement Crisis*. New York: Simon Schuter, 2008.

FARRELL, Nicholas. *Mussolini – A new life*. London: Weidenfeld & Nicolson, 2003.

FAUSTO, Boris. *Getúlio Vargas*. São Paulo: Companhia das Letras, 2006.

FERRAZ, Francisco César. *Os brasileiros e a Segunda Guerra Mundial*. Rio de Janeiro: Jorge Zahar, 2005.

GALEOTTI, Carlo. *Saluto al Duce*. Rome: Gremese, 2001. Tradução para o português pelo autor.

GOEBBELS, Joseph. *Diario 1938*. Milan: Arnoldo Mondadori, 1993, p.144.

GOLGHAGEN, D. J. H. *Goering*. London, 1996.

GOYOS JÚNIOR, Durval de Noronha. *O novo direito internacional público e o embate contra a tirania*. São Paulo: Observador Legal, 2005.

_____. *A OMC e os Tratados da Rodada Uruguai*. São Paulo: Observador Legal, 1995.

GRAMSCI, Antonio. *Il materialismo storico e La filosofia di Benedetto Croce*. Einaudi: Turin, 1948.

GRAMSCI, Antonio. "Ordine Nuovo – 1 marzo, 1924". Apud CANFORA, Luciano. *Gramsci in Carceree il Fascismo*. Rome: Saleno, 2012.

HASTINGS, Max. *All hell let loose – The world at war 1939-1945*. London: Harper Press, 2011.

HIBBERT, Christopher. *Mussolini, the rise and fall of il Duce*. New York: Palgrave Macmillan, 2008.

HILTON, Stanley. *Oswaldo Aranha – Uma Biografia*. Rio de Janeiro: Objetiva, 1994.

HITLER, Adolf. *Minha Luta*. São Paulo: Centauro, 2005 [*Mein Kampf*. Boston: Houghton Mifflin, 1971].

HOBSBAWM, Eric. *How to Change the World – Tales of Marx and Marxism*. London: Abacus, 2012.

138 DURVAL DE NORONHA GOYOS JR.

INCAER, Instituto Histórico-Cultural da Aeronáutica. *A participação da Força Aérea Brasileira na II Guerra Mundial* Available at: <https://www.incaer.aer.mil.br/opusculo_fab_seg_guerra.pdf>.

INNOCENTI, Marco. *Ciano – Il fascista che sfidò Hitler.* Milan: Ugo Mursia, 2013.

KERSHAW, Ian. *Hitler 1889-1936: Hubris.* London: The Penguin Press, 1998.

KEYNES, J. M. *As consequências econômicas da paz.* São Paulo: Universidade de Brasília, 2002.

LIMA, Ruy Moreira. *Senta a Pua!* 4th ed. Belo Horizonte: Itatiaia, 2001.

MAGNI, Laura. *La Storia d'Italia.* Milan: AMZ Editrice, 1989.

MAKIN, W. J. *War over Ethiopia.* London: Jarrolds Publishers, 1935.

MARRONE, Andrea. *La Disfatta Del Terzo Reich – La Battaglia di Stalingrado.* Rome: Newton Compton, 2012.

MAZOWER, V. Mark. *Hitler's Empire.* London: Penguin Books, 2008.

MCCANN, Frank D. *Brazil and World War II: The Forgotten Ally.* The University of New Hampshire. Available at: <http://www.tau.ac.il/eial/VI_2/mccann.htm>.

MONTI, Luisa Sturani. *Antologia della Resistenza.* Torino: Centro del Libro Popolare, 1951.

MOSSE, George. *Le Origini Culturali del Terzo Reich.* Milano: il Saggiatore SPA, 2008.

NETO, Lira. *Getúlio 1930-1945:* Do governo provisório à ditadura do Estado Novo. São Paulo: Companhia das Letras, 2013.

PERAZZO, Priscila Ferreira. *Prisioneiros da Guerra – Os súditos do Eixo nos campos de concentração brasileiros (1942-1945).* São Paulo: Humanitas, 2009.

PETACCO, Arrigo. *La nostra guerra – 1940-1945.* Milan: Mondatori, 1995.

PLESCH, Dan. *America, Hitler and the UN – How the Allies Won World War II and Forged a Peace.* London: I.B. Taurus, 2011.

PLOKHY, S. M. *YALTA – The price of peace.* London: Penguin Books, 2010.

RIBEIRO, Mariana Cardoso dos Santos. "De volta ao inferno. A expulsão de judeus durante o Governo Vargas (1933-1945)". In:

CARNEIRO, Maria Luiza Tucci; CROCI, Federico. *Tempos de Fascismos*. São Paulo: Edusp, 2010.

ROBERTS, Geoffrey. *Stalin's General – The Life of Georgy Zhykov*. London: Icon Books, 2012.

ROGERIO, Dezem. "Hi-No-Maru Manchado de Sangue: A Shindo Renmei e o DEOPS/SP". In: CARNEIRO, Maria Luiza Tucci; TAKEUCHI, Marcia Yumi *Imigrantes Japoneses no Brasil*. São Paulo: Edusp, 2010.

ROSENHECK, Uri. *Olive Drab in Black and White: The Brazilian Expeditionary Force, The US Army and Racial National Identity*. Available at: http://www.academia.edu/1539382/Olive_Drab_in_Black_and_White_The_Brazilian_Expeditionary_Force_the_US_Army_and_Racial_National_Identity. Accessed on: 3rd of Sept., 2013.

RUY E BUONICORE, José Carlos e Augusto. *Contribuição à história do Partido Comunista do Brasil*. São Paulo: Fundação Maurício Grabois/Anita Garibaldi, 2010.

RYAN, Cornelius. *The Last Battle*. United States: Popular Library, 1966.

SÁ MOTTA, Rodrigo Patto. *Introdução à história dos partidos políticos brasileiros*. Belo Horizonte: UFMG, 2008.

SAKURAI, Celia. *Imigração Japonesa para o Brasil. Um exemplo de imigração tutelada – 1908-1941*. Available at: <www.biblioteca.clacso.edu.ar/ar/libros/anpocs/sakurai.rtf>. Accessed on: 1st of Sept., 2013.

SANDER, Roberto. *O Brasil na mira de Hitler – A história do afundamento de 34 navios brasileiros pelos nazistas*. Rio de Janeiro: Ponto de Leitura, 2007.

SARFATTI, Michele. *La Shoah in Italia – La persecuzione degli ebrei sotto Il fascismo*. Turin: Giulio Einaudi, 2005.

SEITENFUS, Ricardo. *O Brasil vai à guerra – O processo do envolvimento brasileiro na Segunda Guerra Mundial*. São Paulo: Manole, 2003.

SEMIRIAGA, M. I. *Missão libertadora das forces armadas soviéticas na Segunda Guerra Mundial*. Rio de Janeiro: Livraria Ciência e Paz, 1985.

SHERRATT, Yvonne. *Hitler's Philosophers*, Yale University Press. Connecticut: New Haven, 2013.

SILVA, Francisco Carlos Teixeira da. *O Brasil e a Segunda Guerra Mundial*. Rio de Janeiro: Multifoco, 2010.

SKIDMORE, Thomas E. *Brasil: de Getúlio a Castelo*. São Paulo: Paz e Terra, 1985 [*Politics in Brazil, 1930-1964: an experiment in democracy*. New York: Oxford University Press, 1967].

SODRÉ, Nelson Werneck. *Formação histórica do Brasil*. 5th ed. São Paulo: Editora Brasiliense, 1969.

STEIL, Benn. *The Battle of Bretton Woods*. Nova Jersey: Princeton University, Press, 2013.

TOGLIATI, Palmiro. *Lectures on Fascism*. London, 1976.

TOGLIATI, Palmiro. *Corso sullivan versari – Le Lezioni sul fascismo*. Milan: Einaudi, 2010.

TOOZE, Adam. *The Wages of Destruction*. London: Penguin Books, 2007.

WERNER, Herbert A. *Iron Coffins*. New York: Bantan Books, 1969.

ZWEIG, Stefan. *Brasil um país do futuro*. Porto Alegre: LPM Pocket, 2008.

INDEX

A

Allies, 10-2, 51, 74, 76, 85, 92, 97-8

Amici d'Italia, 23-5

Aranha, Oswaldo, 65-6, 85, 118

AraUjo, Ernesto, 79

Axis, 9, 26-7, 61-6, 73, 75-6, 82, 126, 131

B

Barbarossa, 9, 50

Basbaum, Leôncio, 54, 56, 119

Battle of Britain, 50

Battle of the Atlantic, 4

Brazil, 7-12, 17, 19, 21, 24-8, 53-69, 74-83, 85-6, 90-2, 99-100, 104, 108, 117, 120-3, 125-7, 129-32

Brazilian Air Force (Força Aérea Brasileira, FAB), 11, 27, 67-8, 74, 77, 79-80, 82, 90, 96, 100-4, 114

Brazilian Armed Forces, 27, 101, 117

Brazilian Army, 27, 67, 85, 89, 94

Brazilian Aviation, 100

Brazilian Communist Party (Partido Comunista Brasileiro, PCB), 58

Brazilian Expeditionary Force (Força Expedicionária Brasileira, FEB), 5, 10-1, 17, 23-5, 27, 85, 87-8, 90-102, 109-2, 117, 126, 131-2

Brazilian Navy, (Marinha do Brasil), 27, 68-9, 77-83, 90

Brazilian Supreme Court (Supremo Tribunal Federal, STF), 119

British Expeditionary Force, 49

C

Campos, Francisco, 56
Carta Del Lavoro, 32
Castello Branco, Humberto, 90
Catholic Church, 34, 37
Churchill, Winston, 8, 66, 88, 121
Ciano, Galeazzo, 36, 58
Civil War, 29, 35, 68, 92, 130
Cold War, 19, 119, 121, 132
Communism, 30, 35, 54
Communist Party of Brazil, 90
Constitution, 55-6, 126
   Brazilian, 119
   Constitutionalist Revolution of São Paulo, 54
   of 1934, 7, 55
   of 1937, 88, 57, 59
   Weimar, 43

D

Divisione Garibaldi, 98
Dutra, Alfredo Soares, 79

E

Empire of Japan, 75
Enlightenment, 30-1
Estado Novo, 8, 55, 57-8, 60, 64, 76, 118-9, 130
Ethiopia, 7, 9, 34

F

Fascism, 25-6, 29-33, 35, 38-9, 43, 54, 57, 61, 106, 119, 124, 130
First World War, 26, 32, 41, 43

G

General Agreement on Tariffs and Trade (GATT), 67, 121
Generals
   Carloni, Mario, 98
   Carvalho, Leitão de, 67
   Clark, Mark, 24, 97, 107
   Costa, Euclides Zenóbio da, 90
   De Gaulle, Charles, 8, 49
   Dutra, Eurico Gaspar, 119
   Farias, Cordeiro de, 90
   MacArthur, Douglas, 107
   Monteiro, Góis, 54, 118-9
   Montgomery, Bernard, 87
   Moraes, João Batista Mascarenhas de, 10, 88-90, 102, 108, 111, 120
   Ord, Gareshe, 86
   Patton, George S., 76, 87
   Pizo Fetter, Otto, 98
      Badoglio, Pietro, 49
      Yamashita, Tomoyuki, 51
German Air Force
   Luftwaffe, 50, 93
German Civil Code, 46
German Democratic Republic (GDR), 125
German Federal Republic (GFR), 125
German Law, 46
Geneva Convention, 76
Giurati, Giovanni, 30
Gomes, Eduardo, 68
Gothic Line, 93
Goyos, Ruy de Noronha, 5, 24, 91, 94, 96-7, 112-3
Great Depression, 32, 43, 109

H

Hiroshima and Nagasaki, 125
Hitler, Adolf, 7, 9, 11, 26, 35-6, 42-4, 46-50, 58, 64, 99, 107, 123
Germany, 8-10, 12, 25-7, 29, 35-6, 41-3, 45, 47, 49, 55, 59-61, 63-4, 66, 68, 73, 75, 85, 88, 98-9, 105-6, 125-6
Nazi Germany, 35-6, 41-52, 58
Hospitals
Nippon Byoin Japanese Hospital, 62
Oswaldo Cruz German Hospital, 61
Umberto I Italian Hospital, 60

I

Integralist Action, IA (Ação Integralista, AI), 58-9
International Law, 25, 66, 120-1, 148-50
International Monetary Fund (IMF), 108, 121
Italy
Fascist Italy, 26, 29-39, 48, 61, 69, 88
Italian Communist Party, 35, 98
Italian immigration, 28
Italian Republic, 18, 24

J

Joint Military Technical Commission, 67

K

Kopp, Theobaldo, 102
Kruel, Amaury, 90

L

Lend-Lease, 10, 27, 67, 77, 82
Liaison and Observation Squadron of the FAB, 102
Lima, Ruy Moreira, 103
Lispector, Clarice, 90
Lloyd Brasileiro, 80, 83
Lojacono, Vincenzo, 59

M

Mafia, 35, 124
Marcondes Filho, 76
Maritime War, 73-83
Martins, Dodsworth, 79
Massarosa, 11, 94
Middle Ages, 32
Molotov, Vyacheslav, 48
Moura, Danilo, 101
Moura, Nero, 100
Müller, Filinto, 75
Mussolini, Benito, 7, 11, 23, 30-8, 48-50, 58, 61, 92-3, 105

N

National Congress, 56
National Constituent Assembly (Assembleia Nacional Constituinte), 119
National Liberation Alliance (Aliança Nacional Libertadora, ALN), 58
National Socialist German Workers' Party, 42, 62
National Union of Students (União Nacional dos Estudantes, UNE), 74
Nazi Party, 42, 44, 62

Nazism, 25-6, 42-4, 57, 130
Nuremberg Laws, 47

O

Onorata Società, 125

P

Pact of Steel, 36
Partigiani, 18, 92, 98, 102, 105-6, 130
Paulista Republican Party (PRP), 54
Pearl Harbour, 9, 51, 66
Petacci, Claretta, 106
Pinto, Heráclito Fontoura Sobral, 56, 75, 118
Prestes, Luiz Carlos, 58, 118
Public International Law, 27, 150

R

Racism, 26, 47, 94
Reale, Miguel, 58-9
Red Army, 10-1, 43, 76, 106
Renaissance, 32
Republic of Salò, 92, 98, 106
Resstel, Rubens, 91, 115
Ribbentrop, Joachim von, 48
Rigo, Robert, 80
Rommel, Erwin, 76
Roosevelt, Franklin, 9-11, 27, 66, 81, 85-6, 121, 131
Russian Revolution, 43

S

Salgado, Plínio, 58-9
School of Aeronautics, 77

Second World War, 8, 18, 25, 27, 38, 49, 64, 69, 76, 82-3, 89, 92, 107, 122, 125, 129, 131
Senta a Pua, 18, 101, 103
Singapore, 9, 51, 107
Socialism, 30, 43
Sodré, Nelson Werneck, 53
Southern Patrol Group, 79
Stalin, Joseph, 107, 121
Szainberber, Salli, 99

T

Trotsky, Leon, 43

U

Unicef, 121
Unification Treaty, 125
Union of Soviet Socialist Republics (URSS), 9, 48
United Nations
    United Nations Charter, 12, 120
    United Nations Conference, 120
    League of Nations, 34
    UN, 81, 120-1, 127
United States of America, 9-11, 19, 24, 27, 43, 51, 55-6, 60, 64-7, 74, 76-7, 79, 82, 85-6, 88-9, 91-2, 96, 101, 104-5, 198, 119, 121-3, 131, 147-8

V

Vargas, Getúlio, 7-8, 10, 12, 26-7, 54-9, 63-6, 70, 74-6, 79, 81, 85-6, 109, 117-9, 122, 130-2
Vasconcelos, José Rebelo Meira de, 103

Versailles
    Versailles Peace Conference, 43
    Versailles Treaty, 20, 41, 43-4

W

Washington Luís, 7, 53-4
Woods, Bretton, 11, 108-9

World Bank, 108, 121
World Trade Organization (WTO), 121, 148

Z

Zhukov, Georgy, 106
Zweig, Stefan, 46, 123-4

ABOUT THE AUTHOR

Durval de Noronha Goyos Junior was born in São José do Rio Preto, São Paulo, Brazil, on 8th June 1951, son of a Brazilian father with the same name and of an Italian mother, Maria Verginia Sabella. He studied in public schools in São José do Rio Preto and in Hartford, Connecticut, USA, as a scholar of the American Field Service. In 1966, when only 15 years old, he was approved in a specialization course in the Italian language and culture, at what is today UNESP, with grade 8, for his thesis "The Aesthetic Conception of Benedetto Croce".

He graduated in law at PUC-SP in 1974 and revalidated his diploma at Lisbon University, in Portugal. He took postgraduation courses in constitutional American law at California University (Hastings College of Law) and at PUC-SP in business law.

He is qualified as a lawyer in Brazil (1974), England and Wales (1999) and Portugal (1989), having founded the law firm

Noronha Advogados in 1978, which now has 16 offices in 8 countries (Brazil, USA, United Kingdom, Portugal, Argentina, China, South Africa and India).

Noronha specializes in international law and has acted professionally in many countries. The Noronha Advogados firm in Miami, founded in 1980, was the first foreign law firm in the State of Florida. The London office, founded in 1988, was also the first Latin American law firm in the City, and this pioneering presence was also to be established in Lisbon (1989), Zurich (1989 – now closed), Shanghai (2001), South Africa (2010) and India (2011).

Noronha acted as a representative of the Brazilian government at the GATT Multilateral Trade Negotiations (the Uruguay Round). He has worked for several other countries, such as South Africa, Argentina, Bangladesh, Canada, China, South Korea, India, Thailand and Uruguay. He is an arbitrator at the World Trade Organization (WTO) and of GATT, of the China International Economic and Trade Arbitration Commission (CIETAC), in Beijing and in Shanghai, as well as the South China International Economic and Trade Arbitration Commission (SCIA).

He has carried out academic activities in various countries, having worked as a lecturer and post-graduation coordinator on the post-graduation program in international commerce at Cândido Mendes University (Rio de Janeiro) and the international law and international commercial law programs of the Paulista Law School in São Paulo. He has been a speaker and lecturer in over 50 teaching institutions in Brazil.

Outside Brazil, in the People's Republic of China (PRC), he has lectured at Shanghai University, Fudam University, the Foreign Commerce University, Tshingua University, Central University and the University of Political Sciences and Law. In India, he was a lecturer at the Foreign Commerce Institute at the Jawarhalal Nehru University (recipient of an academic distinction), at the International Management Institute and at Goa University. In South Africa, he was a lecturer at Wits University, at Cape Town University and at the University of South Africa- UNISA (as a visiting researcher). In the United States of America, he was a lecturer at South Carolina University, Duke University, Miami University (consultant to the North-South Institute), University of Southern California and San Diego University. In the United Kingdom, he has lectured at the University of East Anglia, King's College and the Open University. In Italy, he has lectured at the Trento and Verona Universities. In Portugal, he lectured at the Lisbon University and the Autonomous University of Lisbon; and in Argentina at the University of 3rd February.

Noronha has published more than 750 articles in Brazil and other countries, having collaborated as a columnist on the Sunday edition of Jornal do Brasil for 6 years, until the printed edition stopped publication in 2010. His articles have been published, among others, by Estado de S. Paulo, Folha de S. Paulo, Gazeta Mercantil in Brazil, as well as Pravda and China Daily, in foreign countries, along with many websites such as "vermelho", "la onda" and "última instância", in many languages, including Portuguese, Spanish, English, Mandarin, Russian, Italian and French.

Published many books about international law, such as

- GATT, MERCOSUL AND NAFTA;
- the WTO AND THE URUGUAY ROUD TREATIES;
- STUDIES ABOUT INTERNATIONAL LAW;
- FOREIGN COMMERCE LAW;
- TREATISE ON TRADE REMEDIES;

150 DURVAL DE NORONHA GOYOS JR.

- NEW PUBLIC INTERNATIONAL LAW;
- and NATIONAL AND INTERNATIONAL AGRI-CULTURAL LAW.

On China, he has published:

- CHINA POST-WTO – LAW AND COMMERCE
- GUIDE ON CHINESE LAW;
- and DUSK OF EMPIRE AND DAWN OF CHINA.

On linguistics, he has published:

- NORONHA ENGLISH-PORTUGUESE LEGAL DICTIONARY;
- REMEMBERING PORTUGUESE WITH A DIC-TIONARY OF ANGLICISMS;
- and the MANDARIN PINYIN DICTIONARY.

On the economy, he has published THE DIARY OF THE CRISIS. On international advocacy, he has published THE LAWYER IN BRAZILIAN FOREIGN RELATIONS. On history, he has published THE MARCH OF HISTORY and this CAMPAIGN OF THE BRAZILIAN EXPEDI-TIONARY FORCE FOR THE LIBERATION OF ITALY. Noronha has also published many chapters of books on international law, Brazil, China and economics.

Noronha practices the law and uses professionally the following languages: Portuguese, English, Italian and Spanish. He speaks socially and reads and writes in French. He also speaks Mandarin Chinese socially, reads and writes in Latin and reads in German.

He is a member of the Board of Reino da Garotada de Poá (SP) since 1988; President of the Friends Council of the Confu-